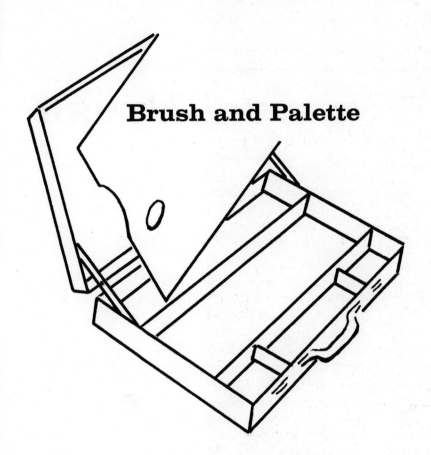

Brush and Palette

Brush

and Palette

PAINTING TECHNIQUES FOR YOUNG ADULTS

Mayo Sorgman

Reinhold Publishing Corporation / New York

For Eleanor, Dara and Bram

Library of Congress Catalog Card No. 65-12975
Designed by BETTY BINNS
Type set by LETTICK TYPOGRAFIC, INC.
Printed by NEW YORK LITHOGRAPHING CORP.
Bound by PUBLISHERS BOOK BINDERY, INC.

Preface

As an art educator and artist, I have long searched for: a book that would give the teen-ager not only basic art principles and technique "know-how," but also furnish him with a background of the great periods of art accompanied by illustrations of great artists, historic and contemporary...an easy-to-follow book stressing the creative philosophy of "individual uniqueness" and showing fine works by young artists...a book that could give the answers to:

"How do I start?"

"What materials do I use?"

"What about techniques?"

"How about framing?"

"What about art schools and scholarships?"

"Where should I exhibit?"

"What careers in art are open to me?"

Well, teen-agers, since I could never find a comprehensive treasury of this type, I decided to write one. And here it is — for you!

MAYO SORGMAN

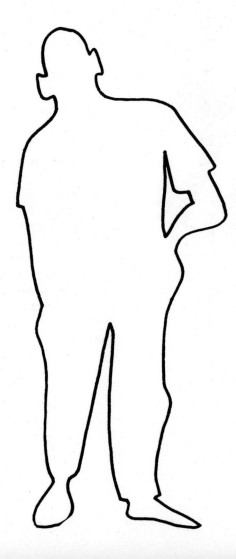

Acknowledgments

Many, many thanks to the following wonderful people without whom this book could not have become a reality:

CLARIS *and* DON BARRON, who started it all;

MISS JENNIE COPELAND, Executive Director of Scholastic Awards, Scholastic Magazines, New York;

MISS LOUISE HOULLIET, Pierpont Morgan Library, New York;

MISS LYNN MAYO, Photographs and Reproductions Department, The Metropolitan Museum of Art, New York;

MISS ELOISE D. MORRIS, Whitney Museum of American Art, New York;

MR. RICHARD L. TOOKE, Rights and Reproductions Department, The Museum of Modern Art, New York;

MRS. CLAIRE MORRISON, secretary extraordinaire;

MR. NICK VERDEROSA, photographer;

MR. ARTHUR WEBER, Spellco Art Supply Company, Stamford, Connecticut;

MR. STERLING McILHANY, a most sympathetic and knowing editor.

My sincere appreciation to the following institutions:
American Museum of Natural History, New York
The Metropolitan Museum of Art, New York
The Museum of Modern Art, New York
Pierpont Morgan Library, New York
Scholastic Magazines, New York
Solomon Guggenheim Museum, New York
Whitney Museum of American Art, New York

Contents

You are not a camera

No, you are not a camera! You are not expected to mirror nature or the things around you; the camera can do that, though in an impersonal manner. For many years the artist was judged solely on his ability to paint things exactly as they appeared. With the invention of the camera, however, the artist lost his function as a recorder of nature. No longer was he needed to portray things factually. This now became the camera's job. At last the artist was free to interpret and paint things as he wished. He could develop his own colors and forms — his own lines and textures. He could create!

Expressing yourself

As an artist, you can use nature to play with, to compose with, to change as you wish. If the sky is blue and you want a green sky — why, paint it green. And if you see two trees in a landscape, but three would look better in your painting, then add another tree. Just as the composer can create a full range of individual effects in music by arranging the notes in a variety of sequences, groupings, rhythms and tones, so can you as a painter reveal your personal thoughts and feelings by your arrangement of the pictorial elements. The important thing is to express yourself in a creative manner.

This philosophy of art is not a new one. Over 400 years ago Leonardo da Vinci stated it this way: "If the painter wishes to see enchanting beauties, he has the power to produce them. If he wishes to see monstrosities, whether terrifying, or ludicrous and laughable, or pitiful, he has the power and the authority to

ONE

You, the artist

(Photo: Nick Verderosa.)

SELF PORTRAIT by Leonardo da Vinci. Sanguine. Palazzo Reale, Turin. (*Alinari-Art Reference Bureau.*)

OLD WOMAN CUT-
TING HER NAILS by
Rembrandt. Oil,
1648. (*The Metro-
politan Museum of
Art,* Bequest of
Benjamin Altman,
1913.)

THE STARRY NIGHT
by Vincent van
Gogh. Oil on can-
vas, 1889. (*The
Museum of Mod-
ern Art,* New York.
Acquired through
the Lillie P. Bliss
Bequest.)

COMPOSITION by
Piet Mondrian. Oil
on canvas, 1921.
(*The Museum of
Modern Art,* New
York. Purchase.)

create them. If he wishes to produce towns or deserts, if in the hot season he wants cool and shady places, or in the cold seasons warm places, he can make them. If he wants valleys, if from high mountain tops he wants to survey vast stretches of country, if beyond he wants to see the horizon on the sea, he has the power to create all this; and likewise, if from deep valleys he wants to see high mountains, or from high mountains deep valleys and beaches. Indeed, what-ever exists in the universe, whether in essence, in act, or in the imagination, the painter has first in his mind and then in his hands."

To reproduce things exactly as they are is merely evidence of good craftsmanship. To copy some one else's painting or to meticulously copy a still life re-quires no great amount of creativity on your part. You are just putting things down as you see them. But to make an original painting, or to interpret a still life in a creative way — through color, composition or tech-nique — that is art!

Just as you learned how to write, to play the piano or the guitar, so you can learn to paint with watercolor, oil, casein and other media. It is a matter of looking, inquiring, studying and practicing.

As you read through this book, you will find many new worlds opening to you. You will be given all the basic elements of painting and aids in learning how to use a variety of media. The rest will be up to you.

Style and technique

The manner in which an artist interprets his subject is called his *style*. Rembrandt's style was naturalistic. You can recognize his painting by the dramatic lights and darks and the glowing, luminous color.

Technique is the manner in which an artist uses his paints and brushes and other tools and materials to express himself. Rembrandt's technique produced a smooth surface; you are not usually aware of the brush strokes. Technique is concerned with two things: the *method* in which the paint is applied — such as alla prima, glazing, scumbling, etc., (more about these later) — and the resultant *density* with which the paint is applied — thick or thin.

Van Gogh's style is expressionistic. He used bright colors and broad swirling brush strokes. His paintings are rough and heavily textured with thick paint. They seethe with movement.

On the other hand, Mondrian's style is abstract. He used pure, primary colors plus black and white. His canvases are smoothly painted and the areas are outlined in black. His works are easy to recognize because of his use of straight lines and blocks of color. They contain the stamp of individuality.

Styles change from artist to artist, from country to country and from one period of time to another. Today, one style that is internationally practiced is Abstraction. As you look at and study paintings in books, magazines, museums and exhibits, you will begin to recognize the styles of various painters and be able to identify their paintings. Styles of paintings are sometimes called "schools" — such as the abstract school or the realistic school. We will discuss this at greater length in Chapter 2, "Points of View."

Every artist develops a style and technique of painting as he works and matures. You, too, will develop a style of your own. Don't try to push or force it; it will come of its own accord and will be as revealing as your handwriting. The way you paint is the sum total of all your experiences. Your intellect and emotions join forces to create a personal point of view. Thus, people will be able to recognize your painting even when you have not signed it. Artists who only copy others or who have nothing individual to say rarely develop distinctive styles. Copyists are "also rans."

Art heritage vs. individual uniqueness

Down through the ages the fine arts have contributed much to man's enjoyment. Painters studying the history of art were sometimes greatly impressed by a specific period or group of artists, or were influenced by a particular style and technique. This influence was revealed in their paintings. However, some contemporary artists, such as the Abstract Expressionists, reject their art heritage and paint only what they feel — today and now. They believe that the only worthwhile aim of the artist is to express his "individual uniqueness," that everything else is secondary. That this is not necessarily so is proved by other artists working in a variety of ways, expressing many beliefs and many more points of view.

A look backward and forward

Let's take a quick backward look, in capsule form, at history and see what artists have painted. Then we'll jet into outer space. Can we predict the art of the future?

Over 20,000 years ago, prehistoric cavemen covered the walls and ceilings of their caves with amazingly beautiful paintings of animals. What inner urge prompted them to paint these animals? We do not know for sure. However, the skill and draftsmanship

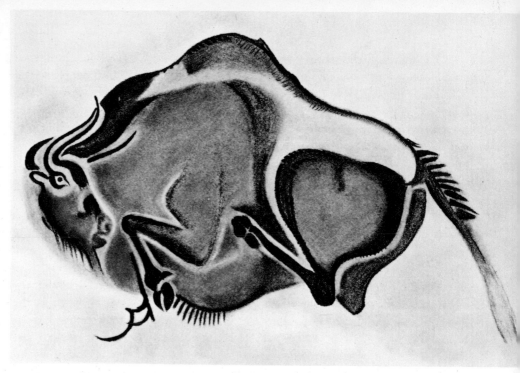

CROUCHING BISON TURNING ITS HEAD.
Cave painting from Altamira, Spain.
(*American Museum of Natural History.*)

they show in their paintings is unequalled even today.

Propelling through the centuries to ancient Egypt, the land of the pyramids and the Nile, we find artists decorating tombs and temples with hieroglyphic writing and flat, two-dimensional, stylized wall paintings. Egyptian art was primarily religious, dedicated to the afterlife.

In Greece, painting was concerned with both religious and everyday subjects. The Greeks depicted their many gods as well as idealized forms of athletes and warriors on vases and frescoed walls.

In the early Christian era and during the Middle Ages painting continued to be primarily religious. Churches were adorned with mosaics and frescoes depicting the events and personalities of the Bible.

Not until the Renaissance, starting in the fif-teenth century, did the artist, in addition to religious painting, begin again to paint other subjects. Then came realistic portraits of noblemen and wealthy merchants. In Italy, mechanical perspective was developed, which brought a new feeling of depth to painting. Landscapes and interiors were introduced as backgrounds to the portraits and religious subjects.

In the seventeenth century, Holland developed a magnificent school of portrait artists who painted not only rich nobles and merchants but also ordinary, everyday people. Some Dutch artists, such as Vermeer, painted richly detailed interiors of homes, while others depicted the landscapes of the Lowlands, broad, peaceful, and serene.

In France, Chardin went into the kitchen to paint the pots and pans and food being prepared. Other artists concerned themselves with mythological subjects, romantic scenes, or protests against social injustice (Goya did just this in Spain). Now there was no subject that could not be painted and considered as art; people of all types and occupations, landscapes, seascapes, still lifes — all became accepted subjects for the artist.

Then at the end of the nineteenth century, the French Impressionists began to experiment with the effects of color and light out-of-doors. From this time on, art became more and more free from preconceived ideas and conventions. No longer did the artist tend to repeat what had been done before. He could paint what he wanted in any manner he chose! In rapid succession there developed a great number of different styles — including Expressionism, Abstraction, Surrealism, and Non-Objectivism. Two of the most important styles today are Abstract Expressionism and Pop Art. Pop artists are fascinated by the possibilities of making "fine art" out of such common subjects as canned food, comic strips, and advertisements and from such familiar signs and symbols as targets and flags.

In this atomic age, through the scientist's microscope, the X-ray, and even from the window of a jet plane thousands of feet above the earth, artists have found new ways of looking at things and points of view that never previously existed. To express man's individuality, artists continue to seek new realities — realities that exist only in the imagination. Since the camera long ago replaced the artist's function to mirror nature, today's artist must paint the world as he understands it — as he feels and dreams about it. And so must you. The time is now!

TARGET WITH FOUR FACES by Jasper Johns. Encaustic on newspaper over canvas, 1955. (*The Museum of Modern Art,* New York. Purchase.)

TWO

Points of view

WE HAVE talked about many kinds of paintings, different styles and techniques. It all adds up to *points of view*.

In order to show you how artists have worked over a long period of time, I shall discuss briefly some of the most important schools of painting. Some you will enjoy, some you may not like — as yet. But as you grow, so will your taste. Your own point of view may be different from any of these, or it may be a combination of several schools. Shall we see?

REALISM

NATURALISM

DUTCH GIRL IN WHITE by Robert Henri. Oil on canvas, 1909. (*The Metropolitan Museum of Art*. Arthur H. Hearn Fund, 1950.)

ABSTRACTION

GIRL BEFORE A MIRROR by Pablo Picasso. Oil on canvas, 1932. (*The Museum of Modern Art*, New York. Gift of Mrs. Simon Guggenheim.)

PORTRAIT OF A YOUNG MAN by Bronzino (1503-1572). Oil on wood. (*The Metropolitan Museum of Art*, Bequest of Mrs. H. O. Havemeyer, 1929. The H. O. Havemeyer Collection.)

IMPRESSIONISM

MADAME CHARPENTIER AND HER CHILDREN (detail) by Pierre Auguste Renoir (1841-1919). Oil on canvas. (*The Metropolitan Museum of Art*, Wolfe Fund, 1907.)

PORTRAIT OF GALA by Salvador Dali. Oil on wood, 1935. (*The Museum of Modern Art,* New York. Gift of Abbv Aldrich Rockefeller.)

SURREALISM

RASALUS by James Brooks. Oil, 1959. (*Whitney Museum of American Art,* New York, gift of the Friends of the Whitney Museum of American Art.)

NON-OBJECTIVISM

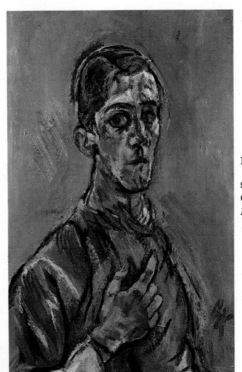

EXPRESSIONISM

SELF PORTRAIT by Oskar Kokoschka. Oil on canvas, 1913. (*The Museum of Modern Art,* New York. Purchase.)

Naturalism

Naturalism is one of the oldest schools of painting. Practiced by the caveman, it continues today, as many of our artists paint in a naturalistic manner. These artists paint the things around them as they see them — easily recognizable with true-to-life color, light and shade, proportion and scale. Portrait painters and painters of seascapes, landscapes and still-lifes usually work in this style. Within naturalism there is a wide range of techniques and individual approaches.

Most contemporary artists first painted in a naturalistic manner before they developed their present style of painting — whether Abstract Expressionism or any other "ism." Naturalism is sometimes called "academism," because it was the style of painting taught in the art schools (academies) where one learned the fundamentals of art. It is interesting to note that Picasso, our greatest abstract painter, started as a naturalistic artist. At the age of 16, in Madrid, he won prizes for naturalistic paintings.

Realism

Realism is very similar to naturalism. The great difference is that a realistic picture is painted in "sharp focus" in contrast to the softer edges, blending and sketchier quality used in naturalistic painting. Realism is a "heightened," sharper naturalism, with detail, form and texture lovingly and painstakingly drawn and painted. This is the type of painting about which one says, "It is so real you want to reach out and touch it."

During the Renaissance, this school of painting was practiced by Italian, Flemish, German and Dutch painters. It was sometimes called *trompe-l'oeil*, or "fool the eye" painting. The artists painted drops of dew on flowers or every hair in an eyebrow.

Our own early American artist, David Harnett, was a great realistic painter. Today in the United States there is a trend back to this school of painting. Artists who paint in this style now are called "Magic Realists." Some of them are Paul Cadmus, Jared French, Andrew Wyeth and George Tooker.

Impressionism

Impressionism is a technique of painting the effects of fleeting sunlight on surfaces. From 1870 to 1880 a group of French artists became intrigued with the beauty of sunlight as it fell on haystacks, fields, churches and lily ponds. They devised a very original manner of painting sparkling and glowing light by placing small brush strokes of contrasting pure colors next to each other. Instead of mixing colors on the palette, these artists left the color mixing to the eye of the observer. A daub of yellow next to a daub of blue emerged from the painting as vibrant green; a patch of red next to a patch of blue, as purple.

The Impressionists, led by Claude Monet, Alfred Sisley and Camille Pissarro, created paintings that shimmered with beautiful color. They had a great influence on other painters of their time. As a result, painting became more lush and colorful. Gone was the academic style with its careful drawing and restrained color in favor of a new brilliance.

Expressionism

Expressionism is a style that emphasizes the emotions rather than the intellect. In this school, the artist paints not what he sees or knows, but what he *feels* about a subject. At the beginning of the twentieth century a group of French and German artists decided to paint in this manner. Their paintings were bold, simplified statements executed with speed. The color was often symbolic, rather than realistic. The paint was thickly applied with heavy black accents added at times. The drawing was distorted and clumsy looking. This was done on purpose! The artist was expressing his personal views of the world. Often the subjects of the paintings were tragic, melancholy and brutal — paintings of protest against man's inhumanity to man.

Ernst Kirchner, Max Beckmann, Emile Nolde and Käthe Kollwitz were German leaders of this style. In nearby Norway, Edvard Munch created haunting paintings and prints in the Expressionist style, while in France, Georges Rouault painted heavy, sombre social protests. Raoul Dufy, Amedeo Modigliani, Henri Matisse and Oskar Kokoschka are other famous artists who painted in the Expressionist style.

Surrealism

The Surrealist school was born in 1924. The members of this group were fascinated by the subconscious mind, by images from the world of our dreams. They made "magic realist" paintings using unrealistic, or dream-like settings. Their paintings contain hidden and secret meanings. They were superb draftsmen and painted so meticulously that usually no brush marks are visible. The color is often symbolic. The artists often depicted a vast, empty space inhabited by strange plants, weird animals and people such as you might expect to find in tales of the supernatural or in outer space. Human bodies are constructed with bureau drawers coming out of them; watches hang in melted shapes from tree branches — all is strange and thought provoking.

Salvador Dali, Yves Tanguy, René Magritte, Max Ernst and Pavel Tchelitchew are among the best known Surrealist painters. Reproductions of their paintings are fascinating to study.

Abstraction

This school, the most important development of art in the twentieth century, was begun by Pablo Picasso and Georges Braque. Their original idea was to reduce all objects to simple geometric forms such as triangles, circles, and rectangles. (This style is sometimes called Cubism.) They did not believe in making realistic representations of things and were interested only in flat surfaces rather than space and rounded forms. They used color as they wished, distorted their drawings and twisted nature at will. They sometimes painted several views of an object at one time and shifted shapes around so that a head might have two noses and three eyes. Picasso and Braque had seen African masks in Paris and were influenced by their abstract shapes.

The abstract movement became very popular, and by 1912 Paris was filled with artists who painted in this manner. Some other famous abstract painters are Juan Gris, Fernand Léger and Marcel Duchamp.

Today, artists such as Graham Sutherland in England and Arthur Osver of this country are still painting in the abstract style.

Non-Objectivism

Non-Objectivism is, as its name implies, "no object" painting. Here the artist is concerned with the relationships of forms and spaces to each other. He is interested in rhythm, unity, balance, and color. In a Non-Objective painting no image or subject can be

Charcoal drawing by Nolan Ross, high school student. (*Scholastic Magazines,* New York.)

seen — neither portrait nor landscape. The *complete* absence of an image is the only thing that distinguishes Non-Objective from abstract painting. To repeat, in an abstract painting a subject is still recognizable, though it may be distorted. In Non-Objective paintings, no image, however slight, can be found.

Non-Objective painting is highly sophisticated and can be compared to "pure music" or modern dance. Some people find it difficult to accept Non-Objective art, since they cannot identify anything in it. However, as Pablo Picasso has said, "Everyone wants to understand art, why not try to understand the song of a bird? Why does one love the night, flowers, everything around one, without trying to understand it? But in the case of painting, people have to understand. If only they would realize above all that an artist works because he must, that he himself is but a trifling bit of the world, and that no more importance should be attached to him than to plenty of other things in the world which please us, though we cannot explain them."

Abstract Expressionism, which is currently enjoying great popularity, is really Non-Objective art. It is emotional rather than intellectual, and, usually, no image is visible.

Important artists in the Non-Objective school are Mondrian, Ben Nicholson, Hans Hofmann, Franz Kline, Mark Rothko and James Brooks.

What is your point of view?

The time is now

Doodle

THE ONLY way to do things is to start — now! Before we explore the individual elements of painting, such as composition, color, value, and line, let's begin with a few simple exercises. What to paint and how to begin? Simple, start by doodling. Any piece of paper and a soft pencil will do. Make six different doodles. Now turn the paper around. Discover anything recognizable? Try adding a few lines; erase an area; rub some lines together with your thumb. Are ideas beginning to emerge? Follow through with other doodles of people, animals, roof tops, TV antennas, the turnpike. Let yourself go!

It is amazing how quickly and simply these scribbles will develop into ideas for painting. Have you seen the Abstract Expressionist paintings done by Jackson Pollock with his "drip" method? Do they look like glorified doodles? Try some of your own. Now make your doodles look like recognizable objects.

Paint to music

Instead of waiting for an inspiration, let's try another device for developing ideas. This time, we'll use pastels and large sheets of paper.

Put on your favorite record and listen to the music. As you listen, let the music tell you what to put on paper. Is the sound swingy or slow, loud or tinkling? What kinds of lines and shapes are sug-

COMPOSITION (4) by Wassily Kandinsky. Oil on canvas, 1914. (*The Museum of Modern Art,* New York. Mrs. Simon Guggenheim Fund.)

gested by the drum beat, the lazy soothing rhythms? Is it a solo, a bass "combo" or an entire orchestra? Maybe thin lines could represent a violin; heavy lines, the deep voiced tuba; red color, the piano; purple, a clarinet. Go on from there. Use your own symbols.

Pencil drawing by David Webb, high school student. (*Scholastic Magazines,* New York.)

Try many quick interpretations. You will find your sketches freer and easier as you listen and work. Study reproductions of the modern Russian artist, Wassily Kandinsky. He made beautiful improvisations by painting to music (preceding page).

Dream and adventure

Carry a small notebook and jot down — in line and shape — your dreams and adventures. Skip the details, just make thumbnail sketches. Here's where to put that visit to outer space, a fantastic nightmare, a trip you are secretly planning. Scribble your thoughts and watch other ideas develop from these. One thing soon leads to another . . . and another. The important factor is to begin — now!

Keep a sketchbook

Take a tip from professional artists. Many of them always carry sketchbooks in which they make notations and drawings of people, places and things. By continually sketching, they develop greater skill in drawing and become more aware of the world around them — be it supermarket carriages, traffic at a stop light or people on a picnic.

Try keeping a sketchbook of your own. In free moments, draw the things you see or experience traveling on the bus, watching a ball game, looking out of the window; your friends, road construction, the hootenanny, the supper dishes in the kitchen sink. The subject matter is limitless. There is a vast treasury of things to sketch. Just look around you. Forget the South Sea Islands and swaying palm trees. Draw the things you know and see. Adventure is where you find it, and it can be right here, at home!

Visit exhibits

If you live in a large city, you can always find an interesting art exhibition or a museum to visit. Make an effort to view as many exhibits as possible. Study other peoples' paintings and see how differently each one works and how each artist portrays his subject matter. Keep watching. The more you look, the more you will see. The more you see, the more you will want to paint. And the more you paint, the better an artist you will be. There may be an exhibit in your library. Sometimes outdoor exhibits are held in the spring or fall.

Read

Many newspapers publish interesting articles on art in their Sunday supplements or daily art columns. Read them carefully and become aware of what is being done in art. It is a constantly changing, new and exciting world.

Magazines such as *School Arts*, *Art News*, *Arts* and *American Artist* are filled with articles and features of interest to you. *Time* and *Life* often have features on art. Visit your library and find the books on art techniques and appreciation in the circulation shelves or in the reference rooms. Borrow books from your art teacher at school. Keep looking at the same pictures, again and again. They will soon become close friends and you will be able to identify the styles of various artists and periods.

What to paint

And now — still wondering what to paint? How about these:

Ink drawing by Richard Piccolo, high school student. (*Scholastic Magazines*, New York.)

Do a portrait. Have someone in your family or a friend pose for you.

Set up an interesting group of hobby items or fruits or flowers to interpret and sketch.

Paint how cold and wet you were during the last snowstorm. Or how happy you were at the dance last Saturday night.

Do you remember the way the lights go on in the city, the look of the beach at low tide, the old grocery store, the supermarket displays, the wonderful advance of spring on the farm? These are only a few subjects for your paintings. What are some others?

FOUR

Building a painting

Oil painting by Jeanette Hori, high school student. (*Scholastic Magazines*, New York.)

"**H**OW CAN you tell whether or not a painting is good?" "Are there any standards we can use to help us judge a painting?" "Is there anything tangible that we can turn to to help us compose a good painting?" These are questions we hear asked over and over again. The answer is "Yes." There are standards to use!

Authority

A painting should be a positive statement. Regardless of the style in which it is painted, it should be a competent piece of work. There should be no evidence of fumbling, corrections, changes or uncertainty. It should indicate that the artist was sure of what he was doing. It should have something to say in a straightforward manner.

Individuality

A painting should express the artist. It shouldn't look like someone else's painting but be the artist's own unique, personal contribution. It should be original! This individuality is seen in many ways:

through the colors used:
> Are they bright, dull, harmonious, "off-beat"?
> Are there few colors, many?
> Are the color areas large, small, blended or separated?
> Are the colors pure and sparkling or muddy and gray?

through the composition:
> Is it ordinary and conventional?
> Does it have an unusual point of view?
> Is it pleasing or disturbing?
> Does it hold one's interest?

through the drawing:

Is it realistic or distorted?

Are the edges hard or soft and fuzzy?

Is the line heavy or delicate, pure or feathery?

through the form:

Is it realistic and solid or flat and abstract?

Is it imaginative?

Is it strong or weak?

through the style:

Is it childlike?

Can it be classified in a particular school?

Is it original and creative?

through the technique:

Is the paint thick or thin?

Are the brush strokes visible?

How is the paint applied?

Are textures used?

Composition

A good painting is not just dashed off — it is first planned. This planning or organization is called composition. Usually artists make several preliminary sketches, or compositions, of a subject until they are satisfied with one that answers their search for a harmony of rhythm, balance and mood. These compositions are rough sketches and are done with no detail. Only the large areas and broad masses of lights and darks are sketched, so that the artist can get the "feel" of the painting.

POINT OF INTEREST

Point of interest is essential to a good painting. There must be one area that attracts and holds your atten- tion. When you take a snapshot, you focus your camera on the important subject and then click the shutter. This same idea prevails in composing a picture. You focus your attention on the main object — all else is secondary.

Where should you place this point of interest in your painting? Almost anywhere except in the center of the picture or too near the edge. Placing your point of interest in the center of the picture divides it into equal areas. This causes monotony and can make a dull painting. To the left or right of the center or above or below it are more pleasing areas in which to place your point of interest. (Where is the point of interest in the painting on page 22?)

Dominance and subordination. By focusing attention on the main subject, you immediately set up a play of dominance and subordination. The subject is dominant. The background and other areas in your painting are subordinate. If you have too many important elements in your picture, it becomes confused and displeasing to the eye.

Dominance may be achieved by making the point of interest larger or darker or brighter than any other part of your painting. Dominance may also be accomplished by painting the point of interest with great detail, leaving the rest of the painting in sketchy form. Or the point of interest may be accented with line while the rest of the painting is not. Study the painting on the opposite page.

BALANCE

A painting should be balanced; it should look "right." A painting may be balanced by the correct proportion of color, line, shape, and texture. As we balance two people on a see-saw, so may we balance our paintings by moving colors, shapes and forms around until they satisfy the eye.

There are two kinds of balance: *symmetrical* (formal) and *asymmetrical* (informal). It is simple to balance a painting through the use of symmetry. In symmetrical balance the two sides of a painting, or the top and bottom, are identical—or nearly so. In asymmetrical balance the two sides of the painting are not identical. Asymmetrical balance is more difficult to achieve, and more interesting. A small area of yellow may balance a large area of blue. A dark spot may balance a large gray area. A shape near the center may be balanced by a small shape near the edge of the painting. Balancing a painting is fun—but it also takes a keen eye, a developing sensitivity and a willingness to make changes as you work.

Look at these small diagrams and see for yourself how dull the evenly spaced areas are. Try drawing these shapes and then make them into sketches of a landscape. Aren't the asymmetrical areas more satisfying?

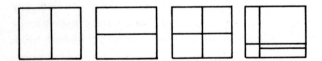

RHYTHM

A painting should have an underlying movement or rhythm, either obvious or subtle. This feeling of movement leads the eye from place to place within the painting. The rhythm is felt through line direction or through the placement of forms, colors, lines, shapes or textures.

UNITY

A good painting should have a feeling of "oneness." No matter how many elements there are in the painting, they all belong together—like children in a family.

Unity is maintained by focusing the attention on one particular part of a painting and by subordinating the other parts. Unity may also be acquired through a limited or harmonious use of color, through a similarity of line, or a repetition of shape or texture.

TYPES OF COMPOSITION

There are many types of composition and I shall discuss a few of them. Look at paintings and reproductions and try to discover how they are composed. You will find this intriguing. Some paintings will be simple to analyze. Others will be more complex and may have two compositions woven together. See how good you are at being a "private eye." Try to find reproductions of the artists I shall mention. They will be eye-openers for you.

CIRCULAR: A circular composition is very rhythmic and has an easy flow of line. It is excellent for happy, active themes. (This composition was very popular in the Renaissance with such artists as Raphael and Rubens.)

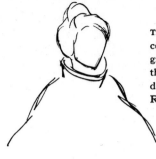

TRIANGULAR: An excellent composition for portraits or a group of figures. (See pediment of the Parthenon in Athens, Leonardo da Vinci's *Last Supper,* or Rembrandt's portraits — page 37.)

ELLIPTICAL: This type of composition has a soaring quality and is most graceful. (See paintings of cherubs by Murillo, Redon's *Silence,* or Picasso's *Girl Before a Mirror* — page 15.)

DIAGONAL: Diagonal composition is very exciting and powerful. (See paintings by Grunewald and etchings by Rembrandt and Goya.)

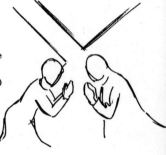

MEANDER: Landscapes with wandering brooks, hills, valleys and fields are naturals for this type of composition. (See paintings by nineteenth-century American artists and landscapes by Hobbema and Constable.)

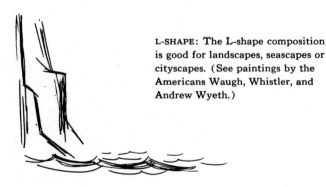

L-SHAPE: The L-shape composition is good for landscapes, seascapes or cityscapes. (See paintings by the Americans Waugh, Whistler, and Andrew Wyeth.)

T-SHAPE: This is almost the reversal of the L-shape. (For variations see Whistler's *Battersea Bridge at Moonlight* and other bridge paintings by Spencer and Stella.)

YOURS: This space is left for you to plan your own composition. It may be different from, or a combination of, some of those pictured. There is no limit to the kinds of compositions you can make.

Compositions can have a psychological impact on the viewer of a painting. You can create a mood by the way you arrange the most important lines or rhythms in your painting.

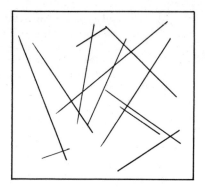

ANGULAR: Angular lines suggest restlessness, excitement and activity. Many of our contemporary painters use angular lines. (See Cubist paintings by Picasso, Gris, and Duchamp, and the violent paintings of such Abstract Expressionists as Franz Kline — page 48.)

HORIZONTAL: This horizontal composition imparts a feeling of quiet, calm and peace. Can you visualize a silent, early morning sea or a long, far-off view of a peaceful valley? Most seascapes and landscapes are horizontal.

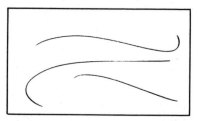

RHYTHMIC: Rhythmic lines symbolize ease, softness, and graceful movement. They are pleasant to live with and keep the eye constantly moving from place to place. (See paintings by Cassatt, Ingres, and Renoir — page 14.)

EXPLOSIVE: This composition symbolizes war, hatred, and chaos. It is frenetic and could be used to depict jazz — the blaze of trumpets or the wail of a blues singer. Try it and see.

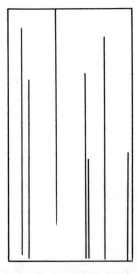

VERTICAL: Vertical lines symbolize classic dignity, soaring skyscrapers, inspirational or spiritual qualities.

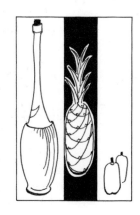

COMPOSING

Set up a still life and interpret it in many ways by using it as a theme in a variety of compositions — vertical, horizontal, circular, etc. You may omit or add things, exaggerate some objects, distort the drawing or change the arrangement in any way you wish. Experiment with variations of line, color and texture.

USING A FINDER

If you paint out of doors and the subject matter is overwhelming and confusing, look through your finder. Move the finder around until you "frame in" what you wish to paint. A finder is simple to make. Take a 6 x 8-inch piece of cardboard and cut out an aperture 4 x 6 inches. That's all there is to it.

Once you have framed an area that looks interesting to paint, make your rough sketches and choose a composition from one of these. Remember: "Finder for focus."

FIVE

All about color

Color is in your eye

EACH ONE of us sees color in a different way. This is because color is in your eye. When light waves of various lengths come in contact with your eye, you experience color.

As you know, white light contains all of the colors of the rainbow, and when the white light is broken up you see specific colors — each of which has a different wave length. Remember when you held a glass prism up to the light and the white light refracted and divided into the rainbow colors?

All objects have a phenomenal quality of absorbing some light waves and reflecting others. For example, a yellow banana absorbs all light waves except yellow ones. These yellow ones it reflects, and so we see the banana as yellow. In like manner, a red coat reflects only red light waves and a blue necktie reflects only blue light waves.

Color has three properties: *hue, value* and *intensity*. *Hue* is the name of a color — red, orange, yellow, blue, etc. *Value* is the amount of light in a color. If a color is light we say the value of that color is high. Conversely, if the color is dark, we say that the value is low. You might have heard people remark that a painting was done in a high or low key. These people were referring, really, to what we call value. A low key painting, or a low value painting, is one painted in dark tones. (Value in this case has nothing to do with money, unfortunately.) *Intensity* is the amount of brightness or dullness in a color. A high-intensity color is considered a bright color, while a low-intensity color is a dull one.

It is entirely possible to make a painting using only one hue (color) with a variety of values (lights and darks) and intensities (brights and dulls). However, most artists use more than one color in a painting.

You can achieve dramatic effects by making most of a painting with low-intensity colors and then accenting it with one or two high-intensity colors. These bright colors would then sing against their dull backgrounds. See for yourself.

The more colors you use in a painting, the more difficult it is to control the harmony. Too many colors in a painting usually reveal the stamp of an amateur. The professional artist uses color with thought and restraint. You can paint a beautiful picture using only three or four colors.

Primary colors

There are three pure colors that cannot be made by mixing. They are red, yellow and blue and are called primary colors.

Secondary colors

Secondary colors are made by mixing two of the primary colors together. Red mixed with yellow makes orange. Red mixed with blue makes purple, and yellow mixed with blue makes green. (See how many different kinds of orange, purple and green you can mix by changing the proportions of the primaries.)

Tertiary colors

The tertiary colors are made by mixing a primary color with its neighboring secondary color. For example:

red + orange = red-orange
orange + yellow = orange-yellow
yellow + green = yellow-green
green + blue = green-blue
blue + purple = blue-purple
purple + red = purple-red

Hundreds of different colors may be obtained by mixing various quantities of two or more colors together. However, the more colors you mix together, the grayer and muddier your colors become. If you want your painting to be fresh and bright, keep your color mixing to a minimum.

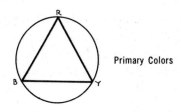

Primary Colors

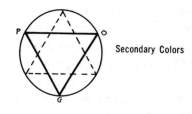

Secondary Colors

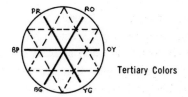

Tertiary Colors

Color harmony

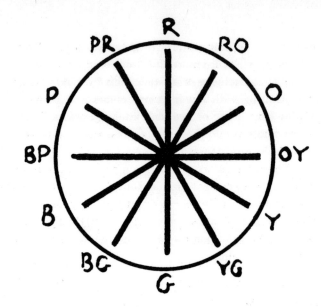

The color wheel is a circle on which the primary, secondary, and tertiary colors have been designated. Various color harmonies may be obtained by selecting specific colors in this wheel.

It is not necessary to use any of these color harmonies in painting your own pictures. You might want to use your own color combinations. But you should experiment with those that follow to see what effects they create. A word of advice: do not use all of the colors in their full intensities!

ANALOGOUS HARMONY   This is achieved by using two or more neighboring colors on the color wheel — for example: red, red-orange and yellow; or green-blue, blue, blue-purple and purple. Analogous harmony is a beautiful, close, rich combination of colors.

COMPLEMENTARY HARMONY   By selecting two colors opposite each other on the color wheel, you get a dramatic, highly contrasting combination of colors, such as red and green, orange and blue, purple and yellow, or red-orange and green-blue, yellow-orange and blue-purple, yellow-green and purple-red. This is a difficult combination of colors to use as you will find. Beautiful neutrals can be obtained by mixing two complementary colors.

TRIADIC HARMONY   Triadic harmony is achieved by making an equilateral triangle on the color wheel and using the colors at each apex of the triangle. Accordingly, one set of triadic colors consists of the primaries: red, yellow and blue. Other sets of triads are the sec-

ondaries: orange, green, and purple; or the tertiaries: red-orange, yellow-green, and purple-blue; or yellow-orange, blue-green, and red-purple. Do not use triadic colors at full strength. Make some lighter and some grayer.

MONOCHROMATIC HARMONY   This harmony has great unity and subtlety. Monochromatic harmony can be achieved by using only one color with or without the addition of black, gray or white. This harmony often gives great distinction to a painting because of its restraint of color. Try painting a seascape in values of green; or green plus white; or green plus white, gray and/or black.

SATURATED HARMONY   To insure harmony in your painting, mix a bit of a specific color with every other color that you use. This procedure will unify all of your colors into a pleasing integrated whole. You might mix (saturate) your colors with yellow for a sunny effect; with blue for a cool, melancholy mood; or with red for a sense of excitement.

You will be intrigued with saturated harmony. It has great creative possibilities. Experiment to discover this wonderful world of color.

LIMITED PALETTE   Instead of using all of your colors, select three or four and paint a picture with them. The use of a few colors is called "painting with a limited palette." Here again, you will find color harmonies that are unified and beautiful. Try painting the same subject several times, each time using a different group of three colors. You will be amazed at the distinctive quality and mood you can capture using this limited palette harmony.

YOUR OWN HARMONY   As we have stated, you do not have to use any of these harmonies but may use any selection of colors that you wish. This will be a "personal" harmony, since you will, no doubt, choose colors that you enjoy. Most artists have favorite colors that are echoed over and over again in their paintings. You can always recognize paintings by Gauguin, Van Gogh, Tamayo, El Greco, Chagall, or Vermeer because of their personal color harmonies.

Grays

Grays may be made by mixing black and white or by mixing a set of complementary colors with white — for example, red and green with white. By mixing the complementary colors, you can get a large variety of grays, some warm, some cool. Mix these complemen-

tary colors and find out how many different grays you really can make. By changing the proportions of the colors you mix, different grays will result. To make a color grayer, add a bit of its complementary color to it.

Black

A color may be darkened by mixing it with black. I do not recommend using black with other colors, however, as it tends to dull them. Instead, try using ultramarine blue or burnt umber or a combination of both for making colors darker.

You can also make your own black by mixing ultramarine blue, burnt umber, and alizarin crimson together.

Black is fine if used alone in small quantities or for accents. As you work you will develop your own feelings about the use of black in painting.

White

When working with oils, casein, tempera, gouache or synthetics, white is used to lighten colors. The more white you mix with your colors, the lighter they will become.

White may also be used as a color, alone, in its own right. The use of pure whites will add sparkle to your paintings and will relieve them of that "heavy-handed" look.

More about color

You can balance your painting by repeating a single color in several shapes or values. You will also dis-

cover that a small area of a bright color can balance a large area of a grayed color — that a small spot of yellow, for example, can balance a large daub of blue. Too many bright colors will make your pictures look harsh and cheap. Similarly, too many dulled, grayed colors will make your paintings sombre. You will develop a "color sense" as you work.

Colors are surprising. They change their appearance because of their neighboring colors. They can become warmer or cooler, brighter or duller according to their nearness to other colors.

Paint nine squares of gray ranging from white to black. After they have dried, paint a daub of yellow over each of the squares. See how the yellow changes as its background is changed. The yellow on white looks much darker than the yellow on black. In fact, it doesn't appear as the same yellow at all. (See chart above.) Try other colors against gray backgrounds, and watch them lose their identities!

Now paint nine squares of red and let them dry. Daub a different color on each of these red squares. What happens to the red squares? Doesn't each square appear to be a different red? As you continue experimenting, you will learn that light colors look darker when they are placed against light backgrounds and lighter when they are placed against dark backgrounds.

Color perspective

The warm colors — red, orange, and yellow — seem to have the power of advancing and expanding when they are used in a painting.

The cool colors — blue, green, and purple — do the opposite. They seem to recede and contract. So, if you want to show distance, use cool colors in the background. This will create an illusion of great depth. Remember how blue the hills and mountains look when you see them from far, far off? And how gray? This is due to the atmosphere between you and the distant view. Objects become cooler and grayer as they recede. As they advance into the foreground they become warmer and brighter. So, to make a color come forward, "warm" it by adding yellow or orange to it; to make it recede, "cool" it by mixing it with blue.

Color vibration

It is interesting to note that when you mix complementary colors together they become gray, but when you put these same complementary colors side by side, they enhance each other and appear more brilliant. For example, if you put bright green next to bright red, the two colors will "jump" or vibrate. This phenomenon can be disturbing to the eye and a draw-

back to your painting. In order to eliminate the vibration, lighten or darken one of the complements and the vibration will cease.

Color symbolism

Artists have always used color symbolically in order to enrich the meaning of their paintings.

The Greeks used green to represent the earth, red to symbolize fire, blue for water and yellow for air. In India, the symbol for a holy man was white, for a soldier, red, and for a slave, black. Chinese brides are symbolized by red, Hebrew brides by yellow and American brides by white. So you see that colors have different meanings according to time, geography and custom.

Color symbolism has been used as an important aspect of religion. The Egyptians used yellow as their sacred color since it symbolized the sun. During the Middle Ages when stained glass was used in the Gothic churches, each color had a specific meaning. In the Christian religion, white symbolizes purity, light, and happiness; red, fire, blood, and charity; blue, the heavens and truth ("true blue"); green, nature and hope; purple, suffering and sorrow; black, death.

In recent years, the German Expressionists and the Surrealists have reintroduced the symbolic use of color. They used color not to depict reality, but to stimulate the emotions. You can make your own set of color symbols. What colors suggest winter, autumn, love, hate, energy, weariness, youth, old age?

Color psychology

Each one of us has his favorite color or colors. Universally, the most popular color is blue, with yellow the least liked. Red is an exciting color. Blue is calm and peaceful, while yellow is gay and cheerful.

Color can affect health and well-being. Too much exposure to red can make you nervous. Blue-green can make you calm and relaxed. (Many hospital rooms are now painted a light blue-green.)

To make a vibrant, dramatic painting you should use exciting colors. To paint a lonely, melancholy picture, what colors would you use? Try making different color sketches of a given theme and discover for yourself the psychological impact of color.

SIX

A line is a line....

AN ARTIST uses line in many ways. He can use it to outline the shape of an object, to divide the areas of his paintings, to show direction. He may also use it to create light and shade, shadow or texture. A line may be brutal or delicate, thick or thin, ragged or smooth. It may be wiry or flowing, of the same thickness or varied. It may be used by itself or together with others. Lines may be straight or curved, angular, whirled, or explosive, fast or slow, rhythmic or awkward, long or short, broken or feathered.

Direction

As we have stated, lines may be used for direction to lead the eye of the observer from place to place in a painting. When you look at paintings, see how the lines move your eyes from place to place, preventing them from leaving the picture. Lines can be used to structure basic composition or rhythm as in this painting by Rubens.

Volume

Lines may also reveal the volume of an object through a variety of ways:

by following the contour of the form

by showing light and shade

by accent

or by ways that only you can create.

WOLF AND FOX HUNT by Peter Paul Rubens. Oil on canvas. (*The Metropolitan Museum of Art,* Kennedy Fund, 1910.)

Psychology of line

Turn back to the chapter on "Building a Painting" and reread what was said about the psychological aspect of composition. The same theory holds true for line.

Lines may express happiness or sadness.

They may be ruthless or gentle,

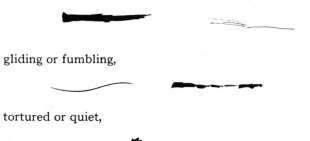

gliding or fumbling,

tortured or quiet,

delicate or bold.

The mood of your painting is revealed by the types of lines you use. Decide on what you want to say and choose your lines accordingly.

Calligraphy

Calligraphy (which means "beautiful writing") is a technique of drawing using a fluid, accented line. The Orientals are masters of this form of art. You should look up examples of Chinese brush painting to share the beauty of this method of expression. The Chinese and Persians have always regarded calligraphy as a great art. In fact, Persian writing is so elegantly designed that it is worthy of framing.

Ink drawing by David Noyes, high school student. (*Scholastic Magazines,* New York.)

Ink drawing by Larry Schultz, high school student. (*Scholastic Magazines,* New York.)

Calligraphic detail from Doe and Deer, Persian Manuscript. (*The Pierpont Morgan Library,* New York.)

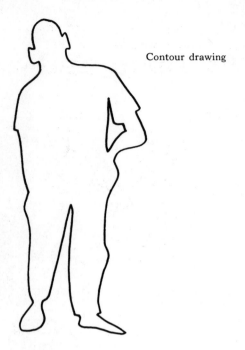

Contour drawing

Curly-cue drawing

Contour drawing

This is an interesting way to draw, particularly if you find it difficult to "break loose" and do anything but tight, overly detailed drawings. It will not only give you freedom of line but will provide a freshness of approach to drawing.

Suppose you begin by deciding to make a drawing of a friend. Gather your materials together and then pose your model. Now take a crayon or brush. Start drawing the outline of the model as you see him. But, *don't look down on your paper or canvas.* Keep your eyes glued on your model and let your arm guide the brush. As you look from place to place on the figure, you will find that your drawing tool will automatically move to create a line following the contour of the model.

Let's start at the head: move down across the shoulders, arms, torso, legs, feet and back up the other side of the model. Do not raise your brush or crayon from the paper. You should be able to draw the figure with one continuous line. Only when you have finished the drawing should you look at the paper. How did it go? Did you achieve the pose? — the proportions?

Now try it again — and again! You will soon discover that by using the contour drawing technique you can quickly catch the pose of a model and the shapes of objects. It is fun to keep a sketch book concealed in your lap and to draw the people around you who are unaware that they are being used as models. Contour drawing will not only give you a sure, fluid line, it will make drawing much easier for you.

A variation of contour drawing is the "curly-cue" technique. Instead of using a simple line, adopt a doodley, curly line. As you draw, these curly lines will add a solidity to your work.

ARTISTS HAVE always been concerned with light, form, and space. With the Impressionists the effect of light was the most important factor in painting. Ever since the Renaissance, much attention has been paid to light and shade, which emphasize and reveal the shape and volume of objects. By varying his treatment of light the artist can depict either shallow space or deep space. Among the masters of light, form, and space are Rembrandt, Leonardo da Vinci, Vermeer and Velasquez. Our Realist painters of today can be recognized by their precise use of these three elements.

Form

Now what is *form*? In the world of art and artists, form may have many meanings. For our purposes, however, form will refer to shape or contour, as in this painting by Cézanne.

Chiaroscuro

Another word you should add to your art vocabulary is *chiaroscuro*. This Italian word means, simply, light and dark. The greater the contrast of light and dark, the more the forms are revealed. The darker the shadows, the deeper the space in a painting. Chiaroscuro was of great concern to the Renaissance artists. It is interesting to note that the Egyptians painted in a very flat manner using no chiaroscuro. The art of China, India, and Japan also reveals little or no chiaroscuro. Our present Non-Objective artists ignore it completely.

No doubt you have seen one of the glowing portraits of Rembrandt with its dazzling lights and shadows. This is chiaroscuro at its peak. On the other hand, a Non-Objective painting by Mondrian or a poster by

STILL LIFE WITH APPLES by Paul Cézanne. Oil on Canvas, 1890-1900. (*The Museum of Modern Art,* New York. Lillie P. Bliss Collection.)

ARISTOTLE CONTEMPLATING THE BUST OF HOMER by Rembrandt. Oil on canvas, 1653. (*The Metropolitan Museum of Art,* Purchased with special funds and gifts of Friends of the Museum, 1961.)

MAMA, PAPA IS WOUNDED! by Yves
Tanguy. Oil on canvas, 1927. (*The
Museum of Modern Art,* New York.
Purchase.)

Toulouse-Lautrec contains no chiaroscuro and is flat,
or two dimensional.

Look at paintings and study how light and shade
were treated by various artists. You will find a great
variety of styles and techniques as each artist uses
chiaroscuro in his individual manner. If he is a contemporary painter, he may use no chiaroscuro at all.

The Surrealists utilized light and shade to depict
a feeling of endless space. Your eye moves on and on
into their paintings, seemingly for endless miles. Analyze paintings by Yves Tanguy and Salvador Dali to
see how they achieved such a great sense of depth.

Positive and negative areas

You have probably heard of the phrase "positive and
negative areas." This is not as mysterious as it sounds.
In painting or sculpture, an object, such as a person,
is a *positive* area, while the space around it is considered a *negative* area. You can easily understand this,
I'm sure. However, some of the abstract painters, like
Picasso, decided that negative areas are just as important as positive ones and proceeded to paint them as
such. In abstract paintings it is sometimes impossible
to tell which areas are positive and which are negative, since they are interwoven with great unity and
design. Look at this painting of *Three Musicians* by
Picasso. Can you determine which areas are positive
and which are negative?

The great English sculptor, Henry Moore, often
puts holes, or negative spaces, in his sculpture. By
looking through these holes we find that the sculpture
achieves a sense of motion. By using holes in his
sculpture, Henry Moore also tells us that negative
space and positive space are interrelated and that
both are important.

When you plan a painting, you will be the one

THREE MUSICIANS by Pablo Picasso. Oil on canvas, 1921.
(*The Museum of Modern Art,* New York. Mrs. Simon
Guggenheim Fund.)

to decide upon how much importance to place on the positive and negative areas.

Source of light

When an artist paints a picture, he usually decides beforehand on the source and direction of the light so that he can achieve unity in portraying light and dark. The Dutch painter, Vermeer, often showed the light coming from a window on the left side of the painting. Tintoretto painted light coming from above or below. Rembrandt, however, put the light wherever he wanted to in his paintings. He would "spotlight" the important part of the painting and leave everything else in shadow. This device gave his paintings a vibrant glow and created great drama. Van Gogh painted a bright blazing light from the burning morning sun or tumbling incandescent stars.

You can choose your own source of light. The light can come from all sides, from the left or right, top or bottom of your painting. Or, like Rembrandt, you can spotlight any part of the painting you wish. It is well to remember, however, that too many sources of light will make your painting confused and lose its unity. So keep the lighting simple! Limit it from one direction.

Remember, too, light creates shadow. But being a creative artist, treat these shadows as you wish. You may eliminate the shadows, exaggerate or minimize them. It's up to you!

Edges

While on the subject of light, we might detour a bit to mention the edges that light reveals. Some artists outline the objects in a painting causing "hard," sharp edges. Ingres used this technique. Other painters, such as Monet, used few, if any, outlines and painted fuzzy, melting, "soft" edges. This imparted a lyric quality to their paintings.

YOUNG WOMAN WITH A WATER JUG by Vermeer (1632-1675). Oil on canvas. (*The Metropolitan Museum of Art,* Gift of Henry G. Marquand, 1889.)

(*Left*) PORTRAIT OF A GENTLEMAN by Jean A. D. Ingres (1780-1867). Oil on canvas. (*The Metropolitan Museum of Art,* Bequest of Mrs. H. O. Havemeyer, 1929. The H. O. Havemeyer Collection.) (*Right*) POPLARS AT GIVERNY, SUNRISE by Claude Monet. Oil on canvas, 1888. (*The Museum of Modern Art,* New York. Gift of Mr. and Mrs. William B. Jaffe.)

EIGHT

Other points of view–perspective

EGYPT

Wall painting: Apuy and his wife receiving offering. Egyptian, XIX Dynasty. (*The Metropolitan Museum of Art.*)

Cassone panel: King Solomon and the Queen of Sheba, Workshop of Sano di Pietro (1406-1481). Tempera on wood. (*The Metropolitan Museum of Art,* Rogers Fund, 1914.)

PERSPECTIVE IS a technique used by artists to show how objects appear as they recede into space. Perspective creates this feeling of space by contributing a three-dimensional quality to a painting. There are many ways of depicting a feeling of space and distance. These methods have varied since the caveman according to time and geographical locations.

Now what are some of the ways artists have used to give the illusion of space? Let's go back to the early Egyptians to see how they created depth in their paintings. As we look at examples by Egyptian artists, we discover that they made no attempt to show deep space; instead, their paintings were flat and two-dimensional. To give some feeling of space, however, the Egyptians placed one object *behind* or partly *overlapping* another. We can see this when we examine Egyptian wall paintings. The artists distinguished someone of importance, a king or a god, for example, by painting him larger than the surrounding figures.

In China and Japan, a different method was used. Space was shown simply by drawing some objects *above* other objects in the painting. There was no attempt to make objects smaller as they receded into the distance.

Mechanical perspective

As you know, when you look off into the distance, objects become smaller, grayer, lighter and less detailed as they move away from you. During the Renaissance, an artist named Paolo Uccello is credited with having invented a system to portray distance. This was called mechanical perspective. Uccello's technique of showing objects in space was enthusias-

RENAISSANCE

MOUNTAIN WAYFARERS by Kuo Hsi. Chinese, nineteenth century. (*The Metropolitan Museum of Art,* Kennedy Fund, 1913.)

tically adopted by other artists of that time and is still used by many artists today. (See page 42.)

Mechanical perspective is concerned with *eye-levels* (horizons) and *vanishing points*. Your eye level is an imaginary line projected from your eyes to the horizon. The eye level or horizon line is where the sky and earth seem to meet. Now this eye-level (horizon) changes in relation to one's height and is, therefore, different for everyone. For example, A and B, two young men, and a talking dog look off into the distance. Tall A says, "The horizon line is up here." Shorty B says, "No, the horizon line is down here." And, the talking dog says, "You're both wrong, the horizon line is down here!" Who was right? All of them, of course! Each has his own eye level. Your eye level is different when you stand on the ground, on a roof, on a mountain, or in a valley.

THE PARIS BIT by Stuart Davis. Oil, 1959. (*Whitney Museum of American Art.* Gift of the Friends of the Whitney Museum of American Art.)

talking dog

Where is *your* horizon line?

Uccello's theory states that:

1. All objects as they recede into space vanish on the horizon line.

2. All parallel horizontal lines vanish on the horizon at points called *vanishing points*.

3. Objects below the horizon come up to meet it.

4. Objects above the horizon come down to meet it.

5. Vertical lines always remain vertical even as they recede into the distance (buildings, trees, people, telephone poles, etc.).

6. Objects originally on the horizon line always remain there.

Two types of mechanical perspective are *parallel* and *angular*. Parallel perspective has only one vanishing point, while angular perspective has two vanishing points—one left and one right. There is also a three-point angular perspective that I won't discuss here. Look it up on your own if you're interested.

In parallel perspective, the horizontal lines are parallel to the horizon line and have one vanishing point called the *center vanishing point*. PROBLEM: Draw a book parallel to the horizon and below it:

1. Draw a horizon line on your paper.

2. Draw the spine of the book.

3. Then project the top of the book to the (imaginary) horizon. Each side of the top will eventually meet at the center vanishing point on the horizon.

4. Decide how big the top should be and draw a horizontal line to determine its size.

5. Now make it look like a book.

6. Erase all guide lines.

7. Try drawing one book on top of another in a parallel manner and see what happens. Can you transform the books to buildings?

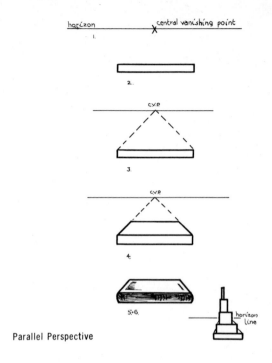

Parallel Perspective

Remember that in angular perspective, we have *two vanishing points* to contend with—one *left* and one *right*. We place these vanishing points at each extreme end of the horizon line. PROBLEM: Draw a book at an angle to the horizon and above it.

1. Draw a horizon line on your paper.

2. Now establish the nearest corner of the book.

3. Project the right side of the book to the *right* vanishing point and the left side of the book to the *left* vanishing point.

4. Determine how big you want the book to be.

5. Project the back of the book to both the *left* and *right* vanishing points.

6. Complete the drawing by making it look more like a book.

7. Erase the guide lines.

Angular Perspective

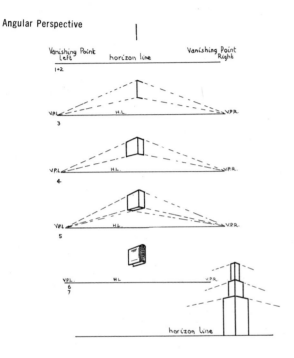

You have noticed that the *vertical* line of the book *remained vertical* throughout, while the *horizontal lines receded* into space. In angular perspective always establish your *vertical* lines *first* and proceed from there. PROBLEM: Draw a city street scene (see below).

1. Draw an imaginary horizon line on the lower third of a large piece of paper.

2. Start with the *vertical* line of a corner skyscraper.

3. Project top and bottom of this building to both vanishing points *left* and *right*. This will establish your street. Since all buildings are parallel to each other on this street, they have the *same* vanishing points, *left and right*.

4. Now establish the *verticals* of *all* the buildings you want to draw.

5. Divide buildings into stores, offices, apartments, etc.

6. Add sidewalks (same vanishing points), street signs, and marquees.

7. Put more skyscrapers in the distance. (If they are not parallel to your street, they will need *different* vanishing points, left and right.)

8. Try adding people, automobiles, and buses.

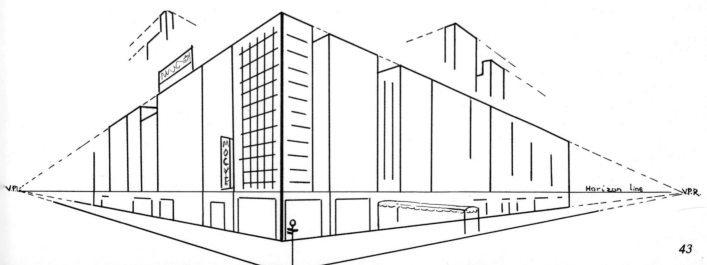

FIGURE IN SPACE by Tom Benrimo. Casein and oil on composition, 1951. (*Whitney Museum of American Art,* New York.)

Contemporary perspective

As we have stated, some contemporary artists ignore mechanical perspective entirely and make little or no attempt to show distance or space in their paintings. This is true of the Abstract Expressionists and of the Non-Objective painters. They are interested only in two-dimensional surfaces.

There are also artists who reverse mechanical perspective and make the objects in the background large and the objects in the foreground small. Other painters follow Cézanne's theory of color perspective:

The warm colors — red, orange, and yellow — advance, while the cool colors — green, blue, and purple — recede. So, in order to make an object come forward, it is painted in a *warm* color; to make it recede, it is painted in a *cool* color.

It is possible to use your own method of perspective. Or you may completely ignore it, if you do not wish to achieve a three-dimensional appearance in your painting. However, try various methods of delineating space; you will eventually find one that will be most expressive of yourself.

STROKE A soft kitten, run your fingers over rough sandpaper, touch a mirror, squeeze a piece of steel wool, rub the petal of a rose; now feel its prickly, spiky stem. What have you been doing? You have been experiencing texture — the feel of things!

Texture is an important element of painting. The right use of texture can enhance the enjoyment of color and form. The lack of textures in a painting may make it monotonous, whereas an overwhelming use of too many textures can be disturbing. In a naturalistic painting, texture contributes a feeling of life. In an abstraction, it provides interest with the varying thicknesses of paint used.

Texture is all around you — in grass, in the bark of a tree, in a crew haircut, in toothpaste, in rocks and sand dunes and in new-fallen snow. Each surface has its unique kind of texture. If you repeat the same object over and over in a painting, it too acquires the illusion of texture. Look for this in textile designs, in photographs of parades, in a pile of marbles or in assembly lines.

Artists have always taken delight in painting textures of fabrics, the sea, flowers, rocks, wood, and skin. The early Flemish and Dutch painters were known for their masterful renderings of surfaces. Some of these textures were so realistic that people were impelled to reach out and touch the paintings. There are artists who plan deliberately to make their textures magically realistic. Their paintings are called *trompe-l'oeil* or "fool the eye." Have you seen any examples of these? Our own American artists, David Harnett and Raphaelle Peale, have made some delightfully intriguing paintings of this type.

NINE

Texture–the feel of things

MUSIC AND GOOD LUCK by William Michael Harnett. Oil on canvas, 1888. (*The Metropolitan Museum of Art,* Wolfe Fund, 1963.)

Black birch. (Photo: Nick Verderosa.)

Pebbles. (Photo: Nick Verderosa.)

Painting textures

Artists choose papers, canvases, and other painting supports having smooth or rough surfaces in order to acquire texture in their paintings. (We will talk more of this when we discuss the individual painting techniques.) Contemporary artists sometimes mix their paints with sand, sawdust or other rough materials in order to get a textural quality.

You can get texture in your paintings by using tools other than brushes. Sponges, twigs, cotton batting, cloth, painting knives, brayers, feathers, and pens are some of the tools that give individual texture characteristics. Try working with these and other tools. Study the textural qualities each of them produces.

Mood in a painting can be conveyed by its textural quality. Would you paint a child with heavy, ragged strokes or a brooding "northeaster" with a series of fine lines? I don't think so! Texture can denote weathered time or brash newness, transparency or murky gloom, silky smoothness or rough, coarse, spikyness. You can obtain textures not only by the use of different tools, but by painting lines or dots in a variety of sizes, shapes, and thicknesses.

Impasto

Texture can be indicated by the use of thick or thin paint. The paint quality of thick paint is called *impasto* and is greatly cherished by the Abstract Expressionists and the Impressionists.

Collage

Early in this century, the Cubist and Dadaist painters became interested in portraying textures beyond those they could achieve by paint alone. They thought, "Why paint a piece of wood, a newspaper, or a piece of cloth when we can get something far more exciting by pasting actual fragments of these things right on the canvas?" And so they did! Bits of paper, fabric, wood, and other materials soon appeared glued to their canvases. These three-dimensional paintings were known as collages — imaginative, orderly arrangements of a variety of materials.

Which do you think is more interesting — simulating textures in your painting or gluing actual textures to the surface?

GUITAR by Georges Braque. Collage: oil on canvas with pasted paper, pencil, and chalk, 1913-14. (*The Museum of Modern Art,* New York. Acquired through the Lillie P. Bliss Bequest.)

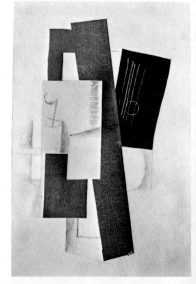

Since the Renaissance

IT HAS been said that oil painting was discovered at the same time in the early fifteenth century by the Van Eyck brothers in Flanders and Andrea del Castagno and Antonello da Messina in Italy. Until that time, artists painted with egg tempera using precise, traditional methods. The Van Eycks, along with their fellow Flemish artists Rogier van der Weyden and Hans Memling, began to use oil glazes over tempera, thus creating jewel-like paintings. The Germans, Albrecht Dürer and Hans Holbein, also worked in this manner.

As the years passed, artists used less and less tempera and more and more oil in their work. In contrast to the small, meticulous tempera panels of the Flemish, the Italian artists painted huge canvases of religious and mythological scenes as well as portraits and landscapes with vibrant colors and delicate gradations of tone. No longer was it necessary to use small brushes which revealed every stroke. Now, wide areas of color were applied with large brushes.

In the sixteenth century, the Venetian painters, the Spaniard El Greco, and the Flemish master Pieter Breugel carried oil painting to new heights. The prolific seventeenth-century artist, Peter Paul Rubens, combined the methods of the Flemish and Italian painters, creating a vigorous, robust technique of his own, quite different from the earlier, tight, detailed panels of the Van Eyck brothers.

From these early times to our own day, oil has continued to be the favorite painting medium of artists. Why is it so popular? How does it differ from the other media we will discuss?

Oil–the universal medium

THE CRUCIFIXION by Hubert van Eyck (d. 1426). Tempera and oil on canvas, transferred from wood. (*The Metropolitan Museum of Art,* Fletcher Fund, 1933.)

VIEW OF TOLEDO by El Greco (1541-1614). Oil on canvas. (*The Metropolitan Museum of Art,* Bequest of Mrs. H. O. Havemeyer, 1929. The H. O. Havemeyer Collection.)

THE HARVESTERS by Pieter Breugel the Elder. Oil on wood, 1565. (*The Metropolitan Museum of Art,* Rogers Fund, 1919.)

MAHONING by Franz Kline. Oil on canvas, 1956. (*Whitney Museum of Art,* New York.)

More about the paint

Oil paint is made of ground mineral, animal or vegetable pigment bound with linseed or poppy oil. It is soluble in turpentine. It is basically an opaque (non-transparent) medium with good covering power. However, it may also be made transparent by diluting it with turpentine or an oil medium.

Unlike water-soluble paints, oils do not dry lighter and so you can visualize your completed painting as you work. In addition, oils dry very slowly allowing you sufficient time for painting subtle relationships of tone and color. The more oil there is in the pigment, the more slowly the paint will dry on the canvas. If you want your oil paints to dry slower or faster, there are additives to mix with the paints to accomplish these ends. (More about this later.)

Oil is very easy to use, very easy to correct and is adaptable to numerous techniques. For the beginner, painting with oils can be messy, but a good supply of turpentine and rags will remedy this simple matter.

Oil paints have always been recognized as the greatest of the art media. Paintings made with oils will last for centuries. Painting with oils puts you in the big league.

Materials and equipment

Colors that fade quickly, or "yellow," are called *fugitive* colors. The colors that I have recommended below are not fugitive. You can be assured that your masterpieces will survive the ages. Here is your list. Later I shall describe each item more fully. (Asterisks indicate the essential colors and equipment.)

Oil Paints in Tubes (artist's grade):

RED	*Alizarin crimson
	*Cadmium red, light
ORANGE	Cadmium orange
YELLOW	*Cadmium yellow, light
	Cadmium yellow, deep
	*Yellow ochre
BROWN	*Burnt sienna
	Raw sienna
	Burnt umber
	*Raw umber
GREEN	*Viridian
	Thalo green
BLUE	*Ultramarine blue
	Cobalt blue
	Thalo blue
BLACK	Ivory black
WHITE	*Titanium white
	Underpainting white

Brushes

Bristle Nos. 2*, 4, 8* (flats)
Nos. 2*, 8, 12* (brights)
Sable No. 6 (flat)
House painter's brush, 2 inch (flat)

Other Painting Tools

*Palette Knife	Brayers
*Painting Knife	Sponges
*Rags	Combs
Twigs	

Supports (painting surfaces)

*Canvas	Cardboard
Canvas-board	Paper
Masonite	Cotton duck
Gesso panels	Burlap (heavy)
Wood panels	Glass

Painting Vehicles

*Turpentine, rectified	*Damar varnish
*Linseed oil, purified	Copal varnish

Other Equipment

*Stretcher strips, wooden (with reinforcement corners — "keys")
*Thumbtacks or staple gun
*Paint box, wood, 12 x 16 inches (cardboard shoebox will do)
*Palette (wood, metal, glass, Masonite or paper)
*Oil cup, double (metal)
*Charcoal (medium) and a kneaded eraser
*Pencil (2B) and a gum eraser
*Fixative and sprayer
*Finder, 6 x 8 inches (make your own)
Stool (portable for outdoor sketching)
Easel (portable)
Table for indoor work

Now read on for further descriptions.

(Photo: Nick Verderosa.)

The paints

Oil paints come packaged in a variety of different-size tubes and are sold in 2 grades, student's and artist's grades. Even though they are more expensive, I would suggest that you buy the artist's grade. It will give much better results. As far as tube sizes are concerned, buy the studio-size tubes, 1 x 4 inches. Since you will use much more white than any other color, it is economical to buy the white in one-pound tubes.

To keep the paint moist and fresh in the tube, the cap should be securely screwed on. If your paint should become hard and dry in the tube, throw it away and buy a fresh one. Sometimes when you are squeezing paint from the tube, a trickle of oil will ooze out. This means that the paint was improperly mixed and ground. If you buy any of the brands I recommend, you should have no difficulty with the quality of the oil paint.

If the small caps become dried onto the tubes, simply strike a match and heat the cap until it is movable.

As oil paint comes from the tube it should be thick. If it is "runny" it needs mixing with the palette knife. To thin thick oil paint, add a drop of linseed oil or turpentine.

All of the oils may be easily intermixed. You will discover a fascinating array of colors as you work. Too much mixing, however, will turn your paint into mud; try to work with bright, fresh color. Mix your own grays and blacks. If you have forgotten how, refer to the section on color to refresh your memory.

You might want to know a bit about the colors you are going to use.

Alizarin crimson is a blue-red. When it is mixed with white you can get a variety of pinks. It has very strong tinting power and a little daub of alizarin goes a long way. It is a good color for glazing because of its transparency. To get rich purples, mix alizarin with ultramarine blue and white.

Cadmium red, light, is a rich, glowing red-orange which combines with cadmium yellow, light, to produce a beautiful orange. You can get a rich brown by mixing it with ultramarine blue. For flesh tones, try mixing cadmium red with white and adding a drop of viridian.

Cadmium orange is a clear, bright color. When diluted with white it loses its brilliance.

Cadmium yellow, light, is a fresh, brilliant color even when mixed with white. It has a powerful tinting ability. Try mixing it with ultramarine blue and white to get luscious greens.

Cadmium yellow, deep, has an orange cast and when mixed with white becomes a good base for flesh tones.

Yellow ochre is an earth color and when lightened turns into a warm beige. It is a good color to use for preliminary sketching on your canvas.

Burnt sienna is an orange-brown.

Raw sienna is a yellowish brown. It is thin and has little covering power.

Burnt umber is a dark brown. When mixed with white it produces a warm gray.

Raw umber is a cool, dark, gray-brown. It becomes a beautiful silvery gray when mixed with white. When mixed with alizarin crimson and ultramarine blue, it turns into a rich black.

Viridian is a cool green with a blue cast. When mixed with white, it turns into a beautiful turquoise. It has little covering power. Since it is thin, however, it makes a good glazing color. Viridian is also quick drying. When combined with yellow, viridian produces fresh, luminous greens.

Thalo green is an acid green. It has a strong covering quality; it is also a powerful tinting agent and so a little goes far. (Watch it!) When it is mixed with yellows, rich greens result.

Ultramarine blue is bright and vibrant, with a slight purple cast. It is rich when mixed with a small portion of white. Too much white, though, will turn this blue milky and weak. To make purple, try mixing alizarin crimson and a bit of white with ultramarine.

Cobalt blue is a true blue that mixes well with white, yellow and the reds on your palette.

Thalo blue, like thalo green, is strong both in covering ability and tinting power. In its pure state, right out of the tube, it sometimes does not appear compatible with your other colors. Dilute it with white or mix it with other hues for best results.

Ivory black is excellent for accents. When mixed with white, however, it turns into a characterless gray. Ivory black dries very, very slowly and is comparatively thin. When mixed with other colors, it has a tendency to kill their brilliance and give them a gray cast. I strongly recommend that you make your grays by mixing complementary and other colors. Experiment to discover how many grays you can mix.

Titanium white is a pure white that has good covering power and is excellent for mixing with all colors. It does not turn yellow but dries slowly.

There are many good brands of oil paints on the market. The following have given me excellent results:

Bocour	Shiva Standard
Grumbacher Pre-tested	Talens
Permanent Pigments	Weber
Sargent Hi-Test	Winsor and Newton

Take my advice and do not purchase a "set" of paints! You will be better off to buy only the ones I recommend. After you have painted for a while, you might want to eliminate some colors from the list and add others. That's your privilege. But for the present go along with me.

Brushes

"I've said it before and I'll say it again," buy the very best brushes you can. In the long run they will prove excellent investments and, of course, will make your paintings so much better. Good brushes last a long time, keep their shapes well, and are sensitive and flexible to the touch. Like an old soldier, a good brush never dies. Even when it is worn down at the edges, it is good for scumbling or for building up impasto.

If you can afford it, have two sets of brushes — one set for the warm colors and the other for the cool ones. This will be useful when you are intensely involved in the excitement of painting and don't want to take time out to clean your brushes thoroughly.

Most oil paintings are done with bristle brushes, though artists today use many kinds of tools to achieve the effects they want. (I recently read of a Parisian artist who likes to daub paint on the soles of his shoes and then walk back and forth over his large canvas.)

But to get back to brushes — bristle brushes are made of stiff white bristles and have long wooden handles. These bristles are much tougher than the soft red sables you use for painting watercolor, gouache or tempera. They hold a good amount of paint and come in three types:

1. "flats" or long-haired with squarish ends.
2. "brights" or short-haired with squarish ends.
3. "rounds" or long-haired brushes with semi-pointed ends.

The flats hold the most paint and are much more flexible than the brights. You can paint long sweeping strokes with them. The small flats are excellent for preliminary sketching and outlining.

The brights, particularly the large ones, are good for fast, direct painting. They can also be used for applying thick paint to the canvas.

The rounds are used for dry brush treatments and for obtaining various textural qualities. (You can do without these brushes, however, so I am not recommending them to you at this time.)

Bristle brushes come in sizes 2, 4, 6, 8, 10, 12 14, 20, 30, and range from 1/8 to 3 inches in width.

You can get wide strokes by using the brush broad-side. And by turning it on its edge, you will be able to produce a fine line.

Practice brush strokes to see how adaptable your brushes really are. Bristle brushes will give a pleasant rough surface to paint. You can either blend the strokes or allow them to show.

The red sable brush is excellent for painting a smooth surface with no visible strokes. This brush is a good one to use for glazing or varnishing.

A house painter's brush will allow you to paint large sweeping areas. It is fine for underpainting.

There are other brushes such as filberts, badger blenders and riggers. After you have painted a year or so, you might want to investigate these.

Your brushes should be cleaned with turpentine and wiped with a dry rag as you change from color to color. When you have completed painting for the day, first clean your brush with turpentine, then under running water rub it into a wet cake of Ivory soap and swirl out all of the color. When you are certain there is no more color in the brush, rinse it in luke-warm water. Squeeze out any excess moisture. Reshape it and lay it flat to dry. You might fold paper crisply around the brush to help retain its shape. When brushes are dry, stack them upright in a jar, wood handles down.

When painting, change from larger brushes to smaller ones as you proceed from broad areas to the final details.

I suggest you use as few brushes as possible. And the bigger, the better! Small brushes will make your paintings look "picky," worked over and amateurish. Be bold! Work large with big strokes! When you wield a large brush, you are forced to paint broadly and to eliminate unnecessary details. I have made successful paintings using only two brushes — a 1/2-inch and 1-inch bright bristle. So you see, you don't have to invest a small fortune in brushes. A few good ones will suffice. And as someone once said, "It's the man behind the brush that counts."

The following brushes are reliable:

Delta	Winsor and Newton
Langnickel	E. H. Friedrichs
Robert Simmons	Grumbacher

Other painting tools

Contemporary artists no longer rely upon brushes

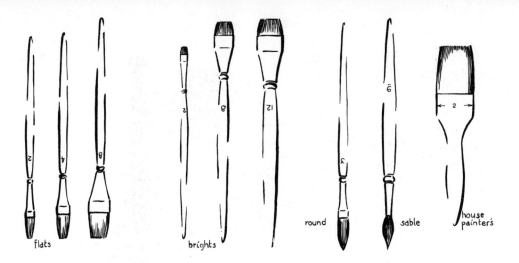

flats | brights | round | sable | house painters

alone for painting. As we have already mentioned, they use any tool possible to achieve the effects they want. Jackson Pollock, the late Abstract Expressionist painter, used to drip paint directly from tubes and cans onto the waiting canvas. Paint may be sprayed, flung, smeared, knifed, rolled, daubed or brushed onto canvas. To help matters, we'll discuss just a few tools to get you started.

NUMBER 27, 1950 by Jackson Pollock. Oil on canvas, 1950. (*Whitney Museum of American Art,* New York.)

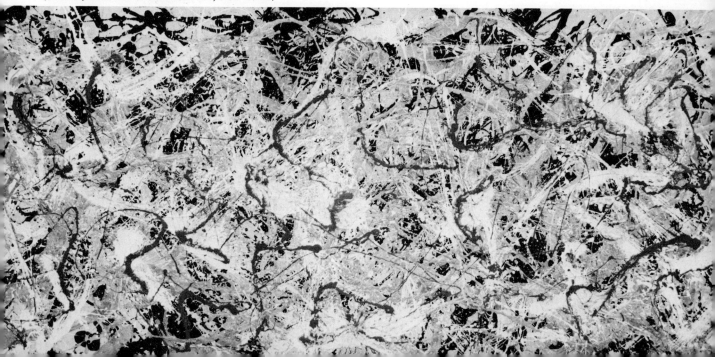

RAGS   Rags may be used in place of, or in addition to, brushes. They are good for smudging broad areas of color. You will also find them useful for glazing.

Soft absorbent cottons are excellent for this. Collect fabrics of various thicknesses, weaves and absorbent qualities. Paint with them and notice the interesting texture each contributes. Every painter needs a supply of rags to be used for cleaning brushes, palette, and the artist himself. Soft absorbent cottons like old sheets, shirts or pajamas are "worth their weight in gold." Save them.

TWIGS   Sometimes you might want to paint a ragged, wiry line. Try using a live twig for this. Apply the paint to the rough end and go to it.

BRAYERS   For laying broad areas of color, you will find a block-printing ink brayer to be most satisfactory. Simply roll the brayer into your oils and use it as a painting tool. I have been able to get interesting effects with the brayer by keeping it comparatively dry and with little paint on it. Using this method on a rough surface will provide you with beautiful textures. When you are finished with the brayer, clean it carefully with turpentine and then soap and water. Roll it on newspaper until you are certain that no paint remains. Then dry it with a soft cloth.

PALETTE AND PAINTING KNIVES   As you work with oil paints you will look upon palette and painting knives as indispensable tools. Many artists paint their entire canvases with knives. Others use the knives for building up textures and heavy impasto. In addition, palette knives can be used for scraping off unwanted wet paint both from canvases and palettes. They are also useful for mixing colors together on the palette.

There are many types of painting knives on the market. Buy the best ones you can afford. Select one with a three-inch-long flexible metal blade. Buy

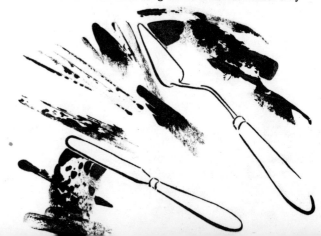

another painting knife with a trowel-shaped blade. The blade should be flexible, but not too springy. A blade with too much spring is frustrating to use, as it will not deposit the paint as easily as you might want. Painting knives are particularly effective when you work with thick paint. Press the knife into the paint and transfer it to the canvas. Use the knife as though it were a trowel. It is possible to apply two or more colors to the knife at the same time and then lay them on the canvas with one direct stroke. By using the knife broadside, a wide stroke can be obtained. Flip the knife on its edge and you can paint a thin, fine line. Every knife stroke will show as you apply the paint to the surface.

When you use knives, you will consume much more paint than you ordinarily would with brushes. (I advise you to save the painting knife technique until you have mastered methods of painting with brushes.)

It is perfectly possible to execute the underpainting with a brush or other tool and over paint with the knife. The painting knife technique will provide a richness and luminosity of color obtainable with no other tool. This technique also offers more satisfying results to the amateur, as it gives a "painterly" touch. Try it and see.

Keep your knives clean; do not allow the oil paint to cake and dry on them. Wipe off used knives with a cloth moistened with turpentine. Then repeat with a dry cloth.

SPONGES Sponges are good for glazing or for applying large areas of thin color to the painting. Saturate the sponge with the thinned paint and daub

away! You can also use a sponge for obtaining textural effects. Pick up thick oil paint with a dry sponge and then apply it to the painting as wanted.

To clean a sponge, drop it into a cup of turpentine. Let it remain until the paint has dissolved. Then squeeze out the sponge and wash it in warm soapy water until it is thoroughly clean. Squeeze out the excess moisture and allow it to dry.

COMBS Save your old combs and use them for producing textures. Apply color thickly to the painting surface. Then, while the paint is still wet, run a comb through it to obtain textural effects. A variety of directions and pressures on the comb will produce interesting textures. However, use this technique sparingly. Too many comb textured ridges will make your painting look busy and overworked. The use of the comb will reveal any underpainting, as in sgraffito. Since wet paint quickly collects on the comb, clean it often.

Paint box

Be economical and use an old shoe box to store your paints, brushes, and other painting needs.

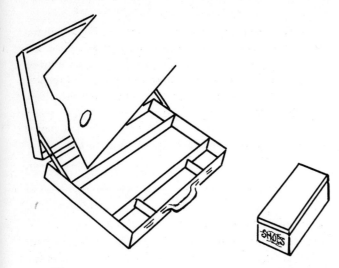

If you want to splurge, however, buy a paint box, 12 x 16 inches. These are made of metal or wood. A wooden box is cheaper. To save money, buy an unfinished one and varnish the outside. Paint boxes have divided compartments. Usually, there are storage places for a palette and canvas board under the lid. A paint box should be large enough to contain your painting materials and yet be compact enough to be carried about with ease. A well-equipped box should contain an assortment of oil paints and brushes, a painting knife and other painting tools, a double oil cup, a palette, a canvas board, charcoal, fixative, eraser, painting media (turpentine, oil, varnish), and a rag.

Easels and stools

You can always use a chair as an easel. Just prop your canvas or panel on the seat against the back. Make sure that you have protected the chair with paper, cloth or plastic to save it from dripping paint. To preserve family harmony and togetherness, it is best to buy an easel of your own.

Basically, there are two types of easels — desk and floor models. Either may be collapsible or rigid. Easels are made of wood or metal. They can be of aluminum — portable and light — or solidly constructed of heavy wood for permanent studio use. Table easels are adjustable so that you may change the vertical angle. Floor easels, too, are adjustable. There is a small ledge on which to prop your painting and a clamp to support the top of your canvas. A good easel is strong enough to support both the painting and your forceful attempts to apply the paint.

If you plan to use an aluminum easel for outdoor painting, anchor it securely by suspending a heavy stone from the center. Otherwise a stiff wind may blow your masterpiece away and texture it with sand, dirt, and grass. Nothing is more infuriating than a portable easel that always collapses when you are in the midst of painting! So be certain that your easel is firm and strong. Make sure all the screws are tight and the moving parts securely fastened before you start to paint.

Look through art catalogs or visit an artists' supply store and examine the types of easels that are available. And while you are about it, look for collapsible stools. These, too, are made of wood or metal and fabric. Some stools fold into unbelievably small shapes. However, if you are long-legged, as I am, make sure that the stool you buy is comfortable to sit on. When you are working out of doors you can sometimes find a rock, a barrel or a stone wall that is more comfortable than a stool.

As a matter of fact, when you paint out of doors, it is best to *stand* at your easel and paint away with verve and freedom. Sitting on a stool is apt to inhibit your movements. In addition, you should occasionally move back from your painting to view it at a distance. You will find that your painting looks quite different when you get away from it.

Canvas

Though there are many kinds of supports available on which to paint, canvas is the most popular. Canvas is made of linen, cotton or a mixture of both. The raw fabric is "sized" with a solution of glue and water. After this is dry, it is "primed" with a coat of white lead paint after which it is ready for use. Linen canvas is much more expensive than cotton; it has a responsive painting surface and is very durable. But for our purposes cotton canvas is more suitable. Later on you can graduate into the linen canvas class.

Canvas comes in a variety of weaves and textures, ranging from a very fine smoothness to a heavy, rough surface. You should select a specific texture of canvas according to the subject you wish to paint. A portrait should undoubtedly be executed on smooth canvas, while a large landscape would call for a roughly textured surface. Practice painting on several different textures and study the effects.

Canvas is sold by the roll in a variety of widths and lengths or by the piece mounted on cardboard or stretchers (more about these later). You can buy canvas either primed or unprimed. The best canvas is imported from Belgium.

Recommended brands of canvas:

Fredrix   Rosenthal's
Grumbacher   U.S. Art Canvas
Lloyd's

For painting, canvas is mounted and stretched on frames of flat narrow strips of wood called stretchers. These stretchers are about 3/4 inch thick and 1 1/2 inches wide. They are notched at each end so that they dovetail, when assembled, to create right-angle joints. Stretchers come in many sizes so that you can assemble them into a limitless number of stretcher frames. Let's say you want to paint a picture 14 x 20 inches. Purchase four stretchers, two 14 inches and two 20 inches in length. Ask the clerk for four wooden keys. (These are small, thin triangular pieces of wood and are free for the asking.) Assemble the stretchers, inserting the keys to tighten the canvas at the corners, and your frame is made. It's as simple as that. Use a steel square and check the corners to see that they form true 90° angles.

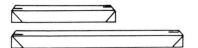

STRETCHING THE CANVAS

You are now ready to stretch the canvas on the stretcher frame. Cut the canvas from the roll (or buy a ready-cut piece) at least 4 inches larger than the stretcher frame; in this instance it would be 18 x 24 inches. This allows you 2 inches on each side to fold around the stretcher. Here's how to do the job:

1. Place the canvas face down on a table.

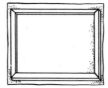

2. Place the stretcher frame over it and center it.

3. Fold the excess 2 inches of canvas over the sides of the stretchers.

4. Fasten the center of the top edge of the canvas onto the stretcher back. (For fastening, use carpet tacks, thumbtacks or a stapling gun.)

5. Pull the canvas taut and fasten the center to the bottom edge of the stretcher.

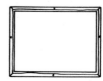

6. Fasten the center of each side of the canvas to the stretcher frame. Make sure the canvas is taut as you work.

7. Now progress to the right and left of each center and fasten.

8. Continue around the stretcher frame keeping each edge at the same fastening stage. Smooth the canvas as you go and keep the same tension.

9. Now fold over each corner, neat and secure.

10. You now have a smoothly stretched canvas.

11. At each corner slip in a key. Push it firmly in place. These keys help keep the stretcher frame in shape. Should the canvas become loose, apply pressure on the keys until the canvas assumes the correct tautness.

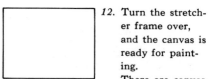

12. Turn the stretcher frame over, and the canvas is ready for painting. There are canvas-stretching pliers available that will help keep your canvas taut as you fasten it to the stretcher frame.

PRIMING

You might want to improve the surface of cotton canvas and make it less absorbent by giving it another coat of your own primer. To do this, buy a can of good white lead paint. Mix it well and thin it with copal varnish, if necessary. Now give the canvas a coat of this white paint. Spread it evenly and thinly with either a large bristle brush or a palette knife. (The knife is preferred.) Allow the canvas to dry for at least a week before using. For extra-rough surfaces, mix sand with your primer. I have always found it good practice to prime several canvases at one time so that I always have an extra prepared canvas ready to use.

DUCK AND BURLAP

To save money, you might want to make your own canvas. Buy a quantity of cotton duck or heavy burlap. Cut it into convenient sizes and attach these to stretcher frames. First apply a coat of sizing (see instructions below). When that is dry, apply one or two coats of white lead *priming* and you're in business. You probably will need to add a third coat or primer to the burlap.

SIZING:

1. Mix an ounce of powdered glue in a pint of water. Stir until the glue is dissolved. Wait until the glue begins to "jel."

2. Spread the "jel" evenly on your canvas with a large palette knife. Allow the canvas to dry thoroughly.

3. If the surface is lumpy, sandpaper it.

4. Re-size with "jel."

5. Allow it to dry — and that's it. Now the canvas is ready for priming.

READY-STRETCHED CANVAS

You can buy canvas already primed and stretched on wooden stretchers or metal frames. These are excellent if you can afford them.

Canvas boards

Canvas is also available mounted on cardboard. These are called canvas boards and are good for painting.

They come in sizes small enough to fit into your paint box, 12 x 16 inches. I do not recommend that you use canvas boards in sizes larger than 16 x 20 inches, as they are apt to warp. Canvases stretched on frames are better for large work.

You can change the surface of any canvas board by giving it an extra coat or two of primer.

Recommended canvas boards:

Fredrix Canvas Panels   Lloyd's Panels

Grumbacher Boards   U. S. Art Canvas Panels

Cardboards

The most economical painting surface for oil that I know of is cardboard. Use thick cardboard and give it two coats of shellac. When this is dry, sand it lightly and apply a coat or two of white lead primer. (This might solve the problem of expense while you are in the initial stages of learning how to paint.)

There are commercial cardboards available that have been stamped to look like textured canvas. I have not found these too satisfactory.

Paper

Many artists enjoy painting with oil on paper. You can too! Try working on unprinted newssheet or heavy papers. Experiment with as many papers as possible and learn how the oil paint reacts to their surfaces. Oil painting papers are available in sheets and blocks. Check with your art store. When you use paper, keep the oil paint comparatively thick. An excess of oil or turpentine will "run" on the paper.

Masonite

Rivaling canvas in popularity as a painting support is Masonite. Masonite can be purchased at lumber yards in sheets 4 x 4 feet, 4 x 8 feet and 4 x 12 feet. Buy the untempered sheets, 1/8 inch thick, and have them cut into the size panels you want. (Masonite panels larger than 30 x 40 inches should be supported with wooden back braces or they will warp.)

You can also buy Masonite panels in the art store already primed. But it is cheaper to make your own:

1. Sand the smooth side of Masonite with sandpaper.

2. Apply two coats of white lead primer. (Allow at least an overnight drying time between each coat.)

3. For a really rough texture, apply a coat of quick-drying underpainting white oil with a palette knife or mix sand with the primer.

The rough side of Masonite has an interesting texture, but it is very absorbent. You might experiment by first applying two coats of glue size to the rough side and then superimposing two coats of primer. Try painting on this and see how you like it.

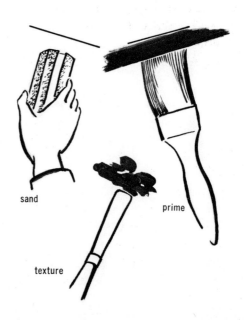

sand

prime

texture

Gesso panels

Gesso panels provide excellent working surfaces for glazing. Refer to page 106 where I describe how you can make your own gesso panels. These panels can also be purchased, fully prepared, in most art stores.

However, I suggest that you give the gesso panels an additional coat of white shellac. This will reduce the absorbent quality of the gesso and prevent the color from "soaking in" when you paint.

Plywood

If you want to paint on plywood, first give it two coats of shellac. Make sure that the first coat is thoroughly dry before you apply the second. Then sand lightly. Sheets of plywood 3/8 inch thick can be purchased at lumber yards. Have the plywood cut into smaller sizes according to your specifications.

Painting vehicles

To thin oil paints and to make them more workable, we use turpentine and oil as vehicles. There are other vehicles that can be mixed with oil paints either to speed or slow their drying time.

TURPENTINE Turpentine is used for thinning oil paints and for cleaning brushes and palette. It is important that you use only rectified or pure gum spirits of turpentine for painting. Turpentine, when mixed with oil, will speed drying. Too much turpentine, however, will weaken the adhesive quality of the paint, so be careful. As you work, you will soon be able to judge the amount of turpentine to use. Another thing, an excessive amount of turpentine will cause your paint to dry with an objectionable surface.

VEHICLES To avoid some of the disadvantages of using straight turpentine as a painting vehicle, mix-

tures have been formulated that are excellent to be used in its stead. Here are formulas of two painting vehicles I like to use:

1. Mix one part of linseed oil with three parts of turpentine.

2. Mix one-third part copal oil varnish with one-third part turpentine and one-third part linseed oil.

Too much linseed oil in the mixture will retard the drying of the paint and will also cause a yellowing of color. So mix these formulas with care.

You can mix a quantity of one or the other of these mixtures and keep it stored in a covered glass jar. When you are ready to use it, stir thoroughly and pour some into the oil cup that you fasten onto the palette.

You can buy prepared painting vehicles in the art shop but they are comparatively expensive. It is cheaper to buy a quart of rectified turpentine and small bottles of linseed oil and copal oil varnish to make your own painting vehicles. I suggest a quart of turpentine, as you will use much of it for cleaning up after painting with your oils.

The less vehicle you use in your paint, the better. And if you paint with a knife, you won't have to use any vehicle at all. For brushing or rolling, you should use just enough vehicle to make the paint easy to handle.

Whenever the vehicle becomes dirty or muddy, throw it away and put a new batch in your paint cup. A muddy vehicle makes muddy paint.

The palette

A palette is a flat surface on which paint is squeezed and mixed in readiness for painting. The colors are arranged in order around the outside, leaving the area in the center of the palette free for mixing.

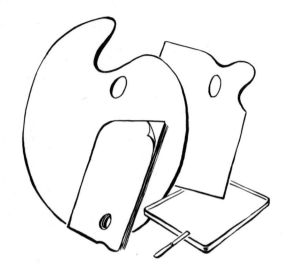

Palettes can be made of wood, Masonite, metal, glass or paper. They come in many sizes and shapes. Some have a hole into which you insert your thumb; the palette is held in one hand supported by the thumb and the crook of the elbow. The other hand is left free for painting. Some artists place their palettes flat on a small table, thus freeing both hands for working. For studio work I like to keep my palette on a small table, but when I sketch out of doors I hold the palette in the crook of my arm.

If you have a paint box, get a palette small enough to fit into its upper lid. Otherwise there is little restriction as to the size or shape you should use. I'm sure you have seen pictures of the traditional oval artist's palette. Today's palettes are more apt to be rectangular in shape. Do not use a palette smaller than 12 x 16 inches, as you will not have enough room for either arranging or mixing colors.

It is easy to make your own palette. Cut out a rectangular piece of plywood or Masonite and give it two coats of varnish so that the oil paints will not be absorbed. An old, flat cookie tin or a piece of plate glass makes an excellent palette if it is placed flat on a table.

There are disposable paper palettes that are particularly good for outdoor work. These palettes are composed of many sheets bound into a pad. When you have finished painting, you just rip off the paper sheet and there is a clean one underneath. Paper palettes are apt to prove expensive because you throw away unused paint when you dispose of the top sheet.

Should you use a wood, metal or glass palette, it is important that you clean the center carefully with a palette knife, turpentine, and rags each time after using. Then wipe it dry.

It is possible to save the unused paint around the outside of the palette by adding a drop of linseed oil to each mound of color. If these deposits of color are left too long they become coated with a thick skin and dry out. Scrape these off with your palette knife.

Always use fresh paint. This is not an extravagance but simply good painting practice. Fresh paint is easy to handle, has a smooth consistency and mixes better.

As you work you will quickly discover how much paint to squeeze onto the palette. You will consume some colors more than others. You will be amazed how much white paint is used, so squeeze a good-size deposit on your palette to begin with. About 1/2 inch of each color and about 2 inches of white is a fair amount to place on the palette.

Use a palette knife for mixing colors. Pick up small quantities of the paints to be mixed and blend them in the center of your palette with the knife. Save the brushes for painting only.

And how do we arrange colors on the palette? — from warm to cool. Since there are more warm colors than cool ones, arrange them on the long, top side of the palette. Place the cool colors down along the left side. White is deposited at the top left corner between the warm and cool colors.

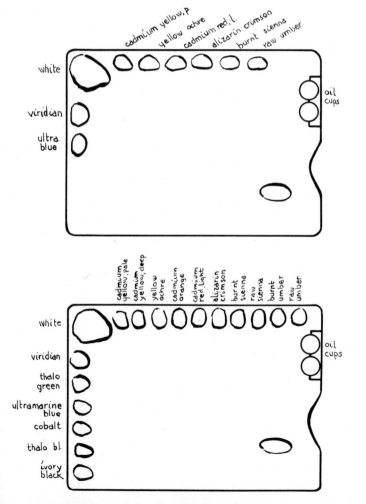

Oil cup

You can buy a double metal clip-on oil cup at any art store. Get one large enough in which to insert a 1-inch brush. (Small empty cold cream jars may be used instead of the metal cups.)

The double metal oil cup is used for holding the painting vehicles. It is clipped to the upper right hand side of the palette. Into one cup pour some turpentine; fill the other cup with the painting mixture (vehicle) you have decided to use.

The turpentine cup is used for cleaning your brushes as you change from one color to another. The vehicle in your other cup is needed for mixing with the paint to keep it maneuverable as you work.

If your palette is kept on a table top, you may also leave your oil cups there for easy access. Remember to keep the contents of the cups clean. Change them frequently.

Finder, pencils, erasers and fixative

For outdoor painting use your finder to assist you in selecting a good composition. Then you should have a 2B pencil with a gum eraser, or some medium charcoal with a kneaded eraser, with which to make your preliminary sketches.

A stick of charcoal is best for sketching on canvas. Lay out only the large areas and leave the details for later painting in with your brushes. This method not only saves time but prevents your paintings from becoming too finicky and "tight."

Canvas is very responsive to charcoal. Any unwanted lines can be eliminated with a kneaded eraser. Sometimes you can break a piece of charcoal and, using it on its side, tone in the masses of blacks and grays. After this is done, spray fixative over the charcoal to keep it from mixing with the oil paints. Then you are ready to paint in whatever technique you choose.

Mixing colors

Reread the chapter on color and review the basic principles of color mixing. Then experiment with oil paints to discover characteristics peculiar to this medium. For best brushing purposes, the oil paint should have the consistency of cream.

You will find when you squeeze the oil paint from the tube that the color is bright and the paint is heavy. By adding white to the tube contents, a remarkable change in the color occurs.

Experiments

1. Squeeze about 1/4 inch of alizarin crimson from the tube onto one side of the palette.

2. On the other side deposit a generous amount of white.

3. With the palette knife, scoop up some alizarin and lay it in the center of the palette.

4. Now wipe the knife clean.

5. Using the knife again, scoop up a bit of white and then mix it with the alizarin already deposited in the center of the palette.

6. By adding more and more white, see if you can mix ten different values (shades) of red.

7. Now try mixing raw umber with alizarin. How many values of dark red can you make? Has the color turned gray?

Mix white and black with all of your other colors. You will discover a multitude of luscious, rich colors by doing this. Any and all of these new colors you've discovered can be mixed with other colors to give you hundreds of hues. But, of course, when painting a picture we use only a few of the mixtures we've found.

Here's an interesting note. You will find that a color looks different on the palette than it does when you paint it on white canvas. And a color will also appear different when you paint it next to or on top of other colors. So you see, painting with color is complex and you must let your eye guide you.

Try mixing the following:

1. Alizarin crimson over cadmium yellow, light; cadmium yellow light over alizarin crimson. Is there a difference?

2. Cadmium orange over cadmium yellow, light; cadmium yellow, light, over cadmium orange. (Now add white to each mixture.)

3. Cadmium yellow, light, over viridian; viridian over cadmium yellow, light. (Now add blue to each mixture.)

4. Yellow ochre over ultramarine blue; ultramarine blue over yellow ochre. (Now add cadmium yellow, light, to each mixture.)

5. Ultramarine blue over alizarin crimson; alizarin crimson over ultramarine blue. (Now add white to each mixture.)

6. Cadmium yellow, light, with burnt umber. (Now add a lot of white.)

You will notice color differences according to the manner and amount of paint used.

Blended area

To paint a smoothly blended area for sky or water, etc., mix up a quantity of basic color — say, blue-green.

Take a large sable brush and saturate it with paint. Then:

1. Make a horizontal stroke across the top of the canvas from left to right.

2. Make another horizontal stroke below this but overlapping.

3. Now add some white to the original color and brush it across the canvas in a horizontal stroke overlapping the stroke above.

4. Keep repeating horizontal strokes as you go lower on the canvas, adding more white to the color mixture with each overlapping stroke.

5. Continue to achieve the desired blending.

Try blending other colors into each other. Paint an area progressing from light to dark. (Sable brushes are best for blending purposes.)

Techniques

Of the many techniques that can be used when working with oils, we shall discuss only a few. You will

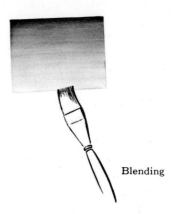

Blending

undoubtedly enjoy one technique more than another. You will also find that it is possible to combine some of these methods. However, don't start adventuring until you feel secure with each of the techniques I shall explain. Then the time will come for further exploration.

Briefly, the traditional Renaissance method of painting began by first making a detailed sketch on the canvas. This was painted over with thin burnt sienna, or another color, allowing the drawing to show through. Then, methodically, step by step, other colors were added — warm over cool, cool over warm, until the artist achieved the effect he wanted. Some of this overpainting was accomplished by the painstaking application of glazes.

In addition, artists have painted *fat over lean*. This simply means that thin, pure paint was applied first to the canvas. When this had dried, juicier paint containing more oil was painted on. The "fat over lean" technique prevented an uneven drying of the paint, cracking and other deteriorations. So, as you work with oil, let "fat over lean" be your slogan.

ALLA PRIMA

Alla prima, or the wet-in-wet technique, is a direct, spontaneous method which has been used for finished work since the Impressionist painters in the late nineteenth century. Alla prima or "all-at-once" painting may be executed with brushes, painting knives, rags or other tools or combination of tools. This type of painting is at its best and most charming when it can be dashed off in one sitting. Because of its speed of execution, it is an excellent outdoor sketching technique. Of course, artists also use the alla prima method for painting in the studio.

But let's go painting out of doors! Gather your fully equipped paint box (with an ample supply of rags), your small, sturdy portable easel and be off. Select a simple scene and with the aid of a finder decide on an interesting composition. Remember, you can change the position, size, shape or color of things as you wish. You are the artist!

If you don't have a finder, try this:

1. Hold up the two fingers of your right hand nearest the thumb. Spread the fingers.

2. Then hold up and spread the same fingers of your left hand.

3. Horizontally cross the two left hand fingers over those in your right hand.

4. You now have an aperture, or finder, through which you can frame a composition.

1. Dip a small bristle brush into turpentine and mix it with burnt sienna to a thin consistency. Use this small brush to sketch quickly the composition on the canvas. Just indicate the large elements, omit details. Wipe off unwanted lines with a rag. Clean the brush.

2. Next, *cover the canvas completely.* Using large brushes and *thin* paint, quickly brush in the sky, the middle ground, and the foreground. Do not attempt to match exactly the colors of nature. Paint the colors you want.

Set up your easel securely so that it can't be blown over by a stiff breeze. When you place the canvas on the easel make sure that it, too, is firmly secured. I once had an almost completed painting disastrously fall in the mud because I hadn't taken time to fasten it on the easel!

Next set up your palette and generously squeeze the paint on it. Clip the oil cup to the palette and fill one section with turpentine and the other with the painting vehicle. You'll use brushes this time? Fine. Select two large and two small ones. Have the bottle of turpentine and some rags handy for keeping the brushes clean. (By the way, I hope you are wearing old clothes because oil painting can be messy!)

You will work standing. This permits more freedom of action and allows you to step back and away from your painting at intervals to see how the work is progressing. You will be amazed to see how different your canvas appears when you look at it from a distance. You will, of course, make many alla prima paintings. With each successive canvas you will become more at ease with this technique and your color will grow stronger and purer, your brush strokes surer.

If you cannot complete an alla prima painting at one time, it is possible to continue working on it the next day. Once the paint begins to dry, however, it is difficult to continue with this wet technique. All set? Now for the action!

3. Now begin using a heavier mixture of paint and paint in the sky. Then brush in the middle ground with large strokes.

4. Paint the foreground — large areas only.

5. Now return to the sky, refining and modifying the color. Do the same to the middle ground and foreground.

7. Work back and forth over the canvas keeping all areas in the same state of progress. As you work sharpen your drawing and light and shade. Work wet paint into wet paint to achieve the blending and colors or textures you need. Occasionally move back from your painting, squint your eyes and look at it. When you do this, the darks will unify, as will the lights, and you can clearly see if your painting is spotty or unified.

6. If there is a color or painted passage you do not like, *scrape it off with a palette knife.* This is very important. When you work in oils, always scrape off unwanted color. If you try to paint over the color without first removing it, you will end up with mud — and I mean MUD.

8. As the painting develops, switch to smaller brushes and add the details. Brush in your highlights and accents.

9. The finished painting.
   (Photo: Nick Verderosa.)

UNDERPAINTING

In contrast to the spontaneous, quick alla prima method, the technique of painting on an underpainting permits the artist to work more slowly, building up his picture gradually over a longer period of time.

An underpainting is the preliminary blocking-in of the painting, which determines the composition as well as such final effects as values, colors, and textures. We will explore three kinds of underpainting:

1. Imprimatura, which is a colored *transparent* glaze.

2. Underpainting with a colored *opaque* (toned) ground.

3. Underpainting for texture with "underpainting white."

IMPRIMATURA   Imprimatura is an underpainting technique of tinting the canvas with a thin (transparent) glaze. This glaze may be of any color or colors (except black). It is used to cover the original white canvas color. You can prepare the glaze by mixing oil color with copal varnish. Mix it well so that the paint is thoroughly dissolved in the varnish. The imprimatura glaze should be applied either with your biggest brush or with a soft rag. Don't worry about applying the glaze evenly, as it will be covered later. Apply the glaze with horizontal left to right strokes. If the glaze is too thin it will run down your canvas; in that event, blot up any excess with an absorbent rag. (You see, in oil painting rags are indispensable.)

It is entirely possible first to make your sketch on the canvas and then paint the imprimatura over it. While the imprimatura is still wet, you can wipe out the areas that are going to remain light, like clouds or sunlit shapes. The imprimatura is used like a watercolor wash. It may consist of one even tone;

it may graduate from dark at the top to light at the bottom (or vice versa); or, it may be a blending of colors. The important thing is to keep the imprimatura *transparent*. Of course, you paint over the imprimatura after it has dried.

UNDERPAINTING WITH OPAQUES   Other methods of underpainting consist of the use of *opaque* (non-transparent) oil paint either for *toning* the canvas in one or more colors, or for making a *preliminary painting* over your sketch. You can underpaint with values of one color or gray, with a warm color or colors, a cool color or colors, or with a combination of warm and cool colors. You may use different colors for different areas.

For best results, this type of underpainting should be used only after you have made several thumb-nail color sketches and have decided on the color scheme of your completed painting. Then the underpainting could be done either in *contrast* to or *similar* to the colors of the completed canvas. The underpainting must be *dry* before you overpaint!

Buy a large tube of "underpainting white" and use it instead of titanium white for the underpainting. This "underpainting white" is quick drying and may be mixed with all of your colors. Light neutral colors with no dramatic, strong darks are good for underpainting.

If you are planning to paint a portrait you might brush the underpainting in with tones of green and overpaint in flesh tones, or first underpaint in tones of gray and then build up the flesh color either with opaque oil or a series of glazes. (We'll discuss glazes next.) Or, you might start out with an underpainting of opaque flesh color and continue with a series of glazes. You see, the variations are many. Through experimentation, you will discover the methods that are best for you.

Here are a few procedures that will help to clarify some methods and reasons for underpainting:

1. Take four 12 x 18-inch canvas boards.

2. Underpaint the first one with an *imprimatura* of reds.

3. Underpaint the second panel with a coat of *opaque* yellow.

4. Underpaint the third in values of blue-green (opaque).

5. Underpaint the fourth canvas board in a combination of opaque colors of your choosing.

6. Allow each panel to *dry!*

7. Paint this *same* seascape over *each* panel: The sky is warm light blue, the water a cool blue-green, the rocks are red and orange-brown. There are two sailboats, one with a white sail and the other with a red sail.

Notice the difference in the results. Did the red imprimatura "glow?" Did the yellow underpainting affect the seascape?

UNDERPAINTING FOR TEXTURE   For textures I like to use "underpainting white" oil paint. When used directly from the tube, thick impastos can be built with it. Very often I apply this thick "underpainting white" to the canvas with a painting knife. It provides a beautifully textured surface on which to work. You can obtain other types of textures by mixing clean sand or other non-disintegrating rough ingredients with your underpainting.

GLAZING

As you learned, a glaze is a *transparent* coat of color. It may be made by thinning oil paint so that it can easily be applied with a brush or rag. You can make your own glazing vehicle by mixing either of these combinations:

4 parts of turpentine with one part of linseed oil, or

5 parts of turpentine with one part of damar varnish.

Mix either of these combinations with the paint and you are ready to glaze. (If you want the glazing vehicle to dry quickly, add a bit of cobalt dryer to it.)

Glazes are used to create transparency and to produce an "inner glow" or depth of color. These effects are achieved by brushing glazes directly over the *dry* underpainting. As used, the glaze is always *darker* than the color beneath. Therefore, if you are planning to work with glazes, your underpainting must of necessity be light in value. You can apply as many glazes over a painting as you wish, as long as each glaze is thoroughly dry before you brush on the

next one. Glazes must be built up one thin coat at a time. To enrich a color, give it repeated glazes of a brighter hue. On the other hand, to "tone down" (neutralize) a color, glaze it with its complementary color. For example, to neutralize green, glaze it with red.

The transparent colors, like alizarin crimson, viridian or burnt sienna, are excellent to use for glazing purposes. However, almost any color may be used for glazing if it has been properly thinned. Glazes are most easily applied with large, red sable brushes or with soft rags. When you glaze, be careful of dripping. The glaze should be smoothly and evenly applied.

Some artists underpaint their canvases in values of gray or some other color. All of the modeling and light and shade are painted with this one color. Then other colors are glazed over the dry underpainting to achieve the effect the artist wants. I have seen beautiful portraits and landscapes executed with this technique. It is one in which great detail can be revealed and accomplished. The glazing technique requires slow, methodical, workmanlike habits. It is also possible to brush opaque oil paint over the glaze and, when that has dried, to continue to glaze some more. Sound intriguing? Then try it!

The fabulous, glowing oils with their wealth of detail of the early Flemish painters were done with this glazing method. Study the works of Van Eyck and Memling to see what I mean.

Another thought — you might have completed an oil painting and then, on second glance, found that there were one or two areas you wanted to warm, cool or enrich. It is possible to make these changes by glazing.

PROJECTS TO TRY

Now for some experiments:

With your oils, quickly paint three canvases of the same New York skyline in values of gray. Wait for them to dry. Then:

With one or more colors, glaze one canvas to depict the early morning light.

With other colors glaze another canvas to reveal New York on a sunlit afternoon.

Glaze the third canvas to represent glamorous New York at night.

Ready for more? On a piece of shellacked cardboard, paint small squares of each of your colors. Allow them to dry. Then glaze one of the squares with red, one with yellow, one with green, one with blue, one with white, and one with black. What happened to the colors when they were glazed?

SCUMBLING

Scumbling is another method of applying paint. It is exactly the reverse of glazing. Instead of a transparent dark color over a light color, you paint a *light* color over a dark one with *thick* pigment. You use the dry-brush technique so that some of the undercolor is revealed. A thick impasto may be built up by scumbling. The Abstract Expressionists are fond of using this technique in their paintings, since it can achieve beautiful color passages.

SGRAFFITO

Sgraffito is similar to scumbling in that you paint over a dried color with another color. However, after applying an even coat of this overlay, you scratch through it with the wooden end of a brush, a twig, or a comb to reveal the underpainting. The line drawings on the early Greek vases were done by this sgraffito method.

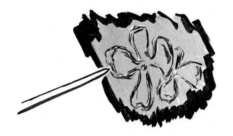

DRY BRUSH

Another method of creating texture is the dry-brush technique. Simply apply paint on the dryish side with a brush or other painting tool by dragging it over the surface of the canvas.

The resulting texture will vary with the amount of pressure you place on the brush, and the thickness and dryness of the paint you apply. After the paint has dried, you can overpaint with another color still using this technique for intriguing results.

Dry brush is superb for old trees, decrepit barns, rocks and other weathered or tortured surfaces.

HIGHLIGHTS

When you brush highlights on an object, never make them pure white. Instead, paint them the lightest possible tone of the object's own color. The Impressionists sometimes painted a medley of colors in their highlights. Other artists, like Rembrandt, built up their highlights with white impasto and then glazed a light color over them. Experiment with highlights and see how a heavy impasto does indeed catch the light.

COMBINING WITH OTHER MEDIA

Interesting results may be obtained by overpainting some areas of your dried oil painting with other media. It is also possible to underpaint with various media and then overpaint, glaze or scumble with oils.

Try combining casein, egg tempera or black India ink with your oil painting. They are very compatible and make exciting companions. (See the chapter on "Mixed Media.")

CORRECTING AND RETOUCHING

It is easier to make corrections in oils than in any other medium. If the paint is still wet and you wish to change the color or drawing, simply scrape off all the unwanted paint with a knife and repaint. Make certain that you scrape the paint down to the canvas. Then start rebuilding your color.

As I previously mentioned, you can warm, cool or intensify a color by glazing. The application of a proper glaze to your canvas if you want to correct a specific passage may save you much repainting.

Varnishing. (Photo: Nick Verderosa.)

If the paint on the canvas is dry, you can make any change you wish merely by overpainting. The only difficulty you might experience would be that of matching a particular texture. But I know you'll be able to cope with this situation, should it arise!

Varnishing

Are you patient, very patient? At least six months after you have completed your masterpiece you can cover it with a damar varnish. This will protect your painting from dirt and moisture and give it a slight gloss. The varnishing should be done in a room kept at a comfortable temperature. Do not varnish on a damp day!

Here are the step-by-step instructions for a good job:

1. Wipe the canvas with a soft brush to remove any dust.

2. Tilt the canvas at a slight angle and let it rest supported on a table.

3. With a large, red sable brush, sweep the varnish across the top of the painting.

4. Continue with horizontal strokes, allowing one stroke to overlap another as though you were laying a wash. Work down the canvas.

5. Use the varnish thin so that the overlapping does not cause a ridge.

6. Do not go back to "touch up" an area.

For a mat finish, use a mat varnish. If you want a glossy surface (and I don't), put on a coat of regular damar varnish. For more gloss, allow the first coat to dry and then apply a second one.

Framing

An oil painting is enhanced by a proper frame. Even though some abstract painters do not use frames, a canvas needs a frame not only for looks and proper support but to prevent it from warping. For your painting, you may use the thin lath stripping that is currently popular or a regular wide frame. Oil paintings do not require wide mats as watercolors do, but they may have wood or linen inserts. In fact, a linen insert is most flattering to a painting.

A frame should not overwhelm a painting by its size, shape, color or intricate detail. It should be in harmony with and echo the mood of the painting. Read the chapter "Framing Your Masterpiece" for more on this subject.

Now you're ready to paint

You've read all about oil painting and have experimented with color mixing and a variety of techniques.

Let's start a painting and follow through. (We'll do this one at home.) Here's a check list.

1. Are you wearing old clothes or a smock?
2. Are there papers or a cloth on the floor around your easel?
3. Is the canvas tightly stretched and firmly secured to the easel?
4. Is the light good (preferably from the north)?
5. Is there space to move back and forth from the easel without tripping over something?
6. Do you have a table on which to spread your palette, paint box, painting vehicles, brushes and tools, rags?
7. Are your brushes and tools clean?
8. Have you squeezed fresh paint in the correct sequence on your palette?
9. Is your double-oil cup filled with turpentine and a painting vehicle?
10. Do you have several preliminary sketches of the composition on a piece of paper?

Good! Now:

Sketch the chosen composition on your canvas with charcoal or pencil.

Remove all excess lines with a cloth, eraser or chamois.

Spray the sketch with fixative.

Keep the mixing of paint to a minimum.

Make the painting *your own* interpretation.

(Check for rhythm, balance, unity and texture.)

Was the painting successful? I'm sure it was.

ROCKPORT SUMMER by Mayo Sorgman. Oil. (Photo: Nick Verderosa.)

Oil painting by Meribeth Duke, high school student. (*Scholastic Magazines.*)

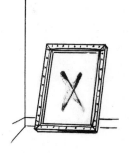

Oil painting by Stella Kowalski, high school student. (*Scholastic Magazines.*)

Now turn your painting to the wall and leave it there for two weeks. Then look at it again.

How does it look now? Any changes needed?

Watercolor — the transparent medium

WOMAN CARRYING CHILD DOWNSTAIRS
by Rembrandt (1606-1669). (*The
Pierpont Morgan Library*, New York.)

THIS IS it! Watercolor, the artist's choice.

It is spontaneous, sparkling, transparent, and fun to do.

Painting with watercolor is considered difficult by some, but it is well worth trying. You will be intrigued by its "wetness" and its ability to depict light, atmosphere and mood.

Because of its quick-drying characteristic, watercolor must be used swiftly and broadly with little attention given to detail. The glow of a good watercolor is the result of the transparency of the medium and the light which is reflected from the white paper beneath the painting.

At one time, watercolor paintings were direct and pure. They were executed with speed and fluidity. Once the paint was applied to the paper, it was never touched — even for corrections. Today's watercolors, however, may be rubbed, scrubbed, incised or painted over. Ink, pencil, gouache and other media are combined with watercolor. Yet the overall impression is still one of transparency.

Watercolor is merely a pigment bound by an adhesive, usually gum arabic. This pigment when diluted with water provides the painting medium. In order to achieve white, you leave the paper unpainted. This adds sparkle to your work.

With watercolor goes adventure! It is a fresh medium that should be treated with a light-handed touch. It is an ideal medium if you like to work out of doors. You can pack a few portable supplies and be off to capture a mood, a scene or an impression that expresses your individuality.

Watercolor has been known since the second century in Egypt. The Egyptians used it for illustrating their Books of the Dead. During the Middle Ages,

BAMBOO, Chinese hand scroll attributed to Su Shih (1036-1101.) Ink on paper. (*The Metropolitan Museum of Art,* Fletcher Fund, 1947, The A. W. Bahr Collection.)

AUGUST LILIES by Charles Demuth. Watercolor, 1921. (*Whitney Museum of American Art.*)

REGION OF BROOKLYN BRIDGE FANTASY by John Marin. Watercolor, 1932. (*Whitney Museum of American Art.*)

SPOOL BED by Andrew Wyeth. Watercolor, 1947. (*Whitney Museum of American Art.*)

monks used watercolor, often embellishing it with gold, to illuminate their manuscripts on parchment. In the fifteenth century, wood cuts printed in black were often tinted with watercolor.

Since ancient times, brush and ink drawings have been executed with high degrees of perfection in China and Japan. These magnificent brush drawings influenced European artists of the seventeenth century who used black and sepia watercolor wash drawings as preliminary studies for their oil paintings. The European artists were entranced by the subtle tones and nuances of reflected light that could be painted with wash. Masterful examples of these wash drawings by Dürer, Rembrandt, and other Renaissance artists are displayed in many museums today.

It was Albrecht Dürer who brought watercolor painting to the stature of great art so that it took its place with oil painting.

In 1800, an important school of watercolor painting was founded by the English landscape painters. They used the watercolor medium to depict their calm countryside and growing towns. Joseph M. W. Turner painted watercolors that were filled with a glowing, mysterious light that has never been equaled.

Modern European painters also have been skillful and imaginative in their handling of watercolor. Cézanne and Paul Klee were particularly inventive.

The Americans were the next to raise watercolor painting to vigorous new heights. Some of our greats? Winslow Homer, John Singer Sargent, John Marin, Lionel Feininger, Dong Kingman and Andrew Wyeth. The best watercolors today are painted in this country.

Materials and equipment

Here is a list of materials you will find useful for painting in watercolor. Each item is described more fully immediately following the list. (Asterisks indicate the essential colors and equipment.)

Watercolors in Tubes (artist's grade)

RED	*Alizarin crimson
	*Cadmium red, light
ORANGE	*Cadmium orange
YELLOW	*Cadmium yellow, light
	Lemon yellow
	*Yellow ochre
BROWN	*Burnt sienna
	Raw sienna
	Burnt umber
	*Raw umber
GREEN	*Viridian
	Thalo green
BLUE	*Ultramarine blue
	*Cobalt blue
	Cerulean blue
BLACK	Ivory black

Brushes
*Red sable, round, Nos. 3 and 9
*Red sable, flat, 1-inch, square end
Bristle brush, ¼ inch (brights)
House painter's brush, 2 inch (flat)
Bamboo, medium

Other painting tools

Rags	Sprayguns
Twigs	Knives or razor blades
Broom straws	Sponges
Brayers	

Watercolor papers
Linen-rag content
Pulp content
Japanese rice paper
Non-woven fabric
Unprinted newspaper
Charcoal paper

Other Equipment
- *Drawing board, 20 x 26 inches
- *Thumbtacks or staples with gun
- *Drafting tape, 1-inch width (or gummed paper tape)
- Paint box, enameled metal, 4½ x 12 inches
- *Water container (pick your own)
- *Charcoal (medium hard)
- *Pencil, (B)
- Kneaded eraser
- *Gum eraser
- Rubber cement
- *Kleenex or rags
- *Finder, 6 x 8 inches (make your own)
- Stool (portable)
- Easel (portable)
- Chair and table, for indoor work

Let's take a long look at the materials you will need so that you can become more familiar with them and learn how they are used.

The paints

Watercolors come in cakes, pans and tubes. You are already familiar with the little watercolor pans you used in school. Cake watercolors have a tendency to dry and crack. In addition, you sometimes have to dig into them with your brush in order to release an adequate amount of paint.

Tube watercolors are the easiest and best to use. You can squeeze enough paint into your paint box palette to assure freedom and ease in loading your brush full of color as you need it. Tube colors will also supply you with clean, juicy, moist paint. If you keep the caps securely screwed on these tubes, the watercolor within will remain fresh and will not harden. Sometimes you may find that the little caps

(Photo: Nick Verderosa.)

have stuck tight. Heat them with a match and they will quickly loosen, or run them under hot water for a moment.

I have listed 16 colors for you, but you can paint very well with the minimum 10 I have starred. There are many more colors available, but you will be able to paint almost anything with this selection. In fact, the fewer colors you use, the more harmonious your painting is apt to be. As you gain experience and proficiency, you may later wish to supplement this list with other colors of your own choice.

The colors recommended are permanent ones and will not fade. They may be mixed with each other. You will notice that there is no white, gray or purple suggested. Since white pigment is opaque, mixing it with your watercolors will make them opaque also and will rob them of their brilliance. So no white! You can mix your own purples or grays by using some of the colors on the list (more about this later).

Tube watercolors are sold as student's or artist's colors. Even though they are a little more expensive, buy the artist's colors. They are much more fluid to use, have richer color and will give you excellent results for your efforts.

The following brands are good: Grumbacher, Permanent Pigments, Shiva, and Winsor and Newton.

There are other brands, but these are the ones that have given me satisfaction over a long period of time. Don't buy a set of watercolors. Buy only the colors recommended.

Brushes

Good brushes are indispensable to the watercolorist. Here is where you should splurge and purchase the very best you can afford. A good brush will not only perform beautifully for you, but will last for years; it is an excellent investment.

Before buying a brush, give it the "flexible and springy" test. Dip it in water and see if it retains its shape and resiliency. Flat brushes should remain firm so that you can paint either a broad stroke or a thin line with them. A round brush should come to a point if you revolve the tip in the palm of your hand. If it turns into a mop when it is immersed in water, it is a poor brush indeed.

Recommended brands are Langnickel, Delta, Robert Simmons, Winsor and Newton, Grumbacher.

You do not need many brushes to paint with watercolor. In fact, the three I recommended will get you started. With a flick of the wrist, you will learn to coax many types of lines from a single brush. The fewer brushes you use, the less finicky your painting will be; the bigger the brush, the broader and freer your painting.

Two round, red sable brushes—a small No. 3 and a large No. 9—will equip you to paint both large areas and small details. A one-inch, flat, red sable

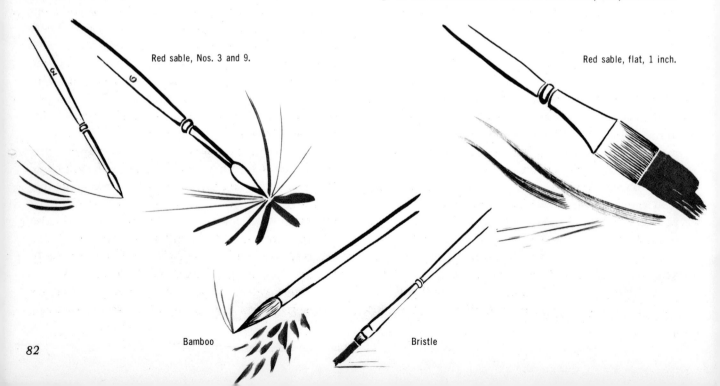

Red sable, Nos. 3 and 9.

Red sable, flat, 1 inch.

Bamboo

Bristle

with a square end will complete this trio of essential brushes. The flat brush will enable you to paint skies and large washes. This brush is extremely versatile. By using its broad side, you can paint a wide swath. By turning it on its edge, you can produce an amazingly thin line. In fact, I have painted a complete watercolor with this one brush.

A bright bristle brush, 1/4 inch wide, can be used for dry brush techniques or for scrubbing out color. Bristle brushes are normally used for oil painting. They have long handles and stiff white brushes.

The two-inch flat housepainter's brush will enable you to sweep a color area across the paper in one mighty stroke. Some artists use even larger brushes, but I'm certain that this two-incher will be adequate for you.

To clean your brushes, wash them in soapy water and rinse. Do not use hot water!

House painter's, 2 inch.

HOUSE AMONG TREES by Paul Cézanne. Watercolor, 1890-1900. (*The Museum of Modern Art,* New York. Lillie P. Bliss Collection.)

Other painting tools

The contemporary artist does not always adhere to traditional methods or techniques of painting but is always seeking new and varied means of expression. In addition to, or instead of, brushes, he uses rags, twigs, broom straws, brayers, sprayguns, and even his fingers to achieve a particular effect. By experimenting with some of these suggested devices, you will find out what happens when they are used separately or in combination with each other.

RAGS Various textural effects are contributed by different types of rags. You may paint smooth surfaces with fine cottons, or stippled and dry-brush effects with coarser and less absorbent fabrics. Gather a good supply of rags; they are also invaluable for cleaning your brushes and paint box.

TWIGS For a ragged, wiry line, try painting with a twig broken from a tree or bush. Use the rough end of the twig, saturate it with paint and let yourself go.

BROOM STRAWS To get a very delicate, scratchy line or textural effect, try using ordinary broom straws. Have several handy, for, as they become wet and too flexible, they have to be replaced with stiff dry ones.

BRAYERS If you wish to lay a broad area of color that has a textural quality, roll an ordinary block-printing brayer into your color and use it for painting. According to the weight and surface of the paper and the moistness of your paint, various effects may be obtained. You will find the brayer particularly good for painting abstracts.

SPRAYGUNS These may be used for spraying fine, graded tones of color on the paper. However, overuse of the spraygun may impart a "commercial" look to your painting. Use this device with moderation.

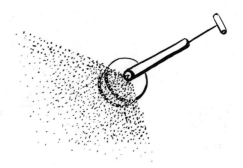

KNIVES Sharp knives or razor blades (single-edge for safety) may be used to scratch out white lines from dark areas. You can use these tools on either wet or dry papers if you are careful. If you are painting white birch trees or light boat masts

against a dark sky, you could first wash in the sky and then pick out the lights you wanted with your knife or blade. You can also pick out dancing highlights on dark waves in this manner. The heavier the paper on which you paint, the easier it will be to scratch out white accents. Extreme care should be taken not to cut through the paper; merely scratch the surface.

SPONGES You may either paint with sponges or use them to blot up excess water or unwanted color. If you want to lighten a color area on the paper,

you might try a sponge. Do not rub too hard or too deeply as you will disturb the surface of the paper and cause a matted look. A small 5-inch sponge is a good size to have.

Watercolor papers

Standard watercolor papers come in sheets 22 x 30 inches. Blocks of watercolor paper are also available and come in a variety of sizes from 9 x 12 inches to 18 x 24 inches. There are usually 24 sheets in a block. Painting on a watercolor block eliminates the need of a drawing board.

For making color notes or quick sketches, you can purchase inexpensive, spiral-bound watercolor paper books.

The kind of paper you use determines the character of your completed watercolor. If you are aiming for sparkle and glitter, use heavily textured surfaces. The pigment will adhere to the top of the grain leaving the depressions white. For laying large areas of wash or graded tones, smoother papers are more desirable.

Since you mix your pigment with water for painting, a good watercolor paper must be able to absorb excess moisture when wet without wrinkling or buckling. (To prevent this buckling from occurring, you sometimes must stretch the watercolor paper before painting on it. More about this later.)

Watercolor paper is made in many qualities, weights, and textures. You should select those papers that will not buckle when wet. They should have enough "tooth" or grain to hold the paint and prevent it from sliding off into a puddle. Obviously, slick surfaces do not lend themselves to watercolor painting.

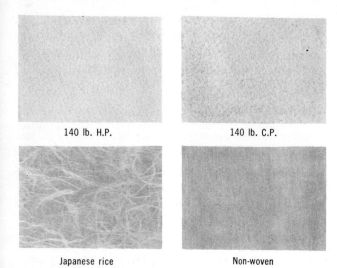

| 140 lb. H.P. | 140 lb. C.P. |

| Japanese rice | Non-woven |

Good papers are absorbent enough to hold the paint, and yet not too absorbent to act as blotters. The best and most expensive papers are those having a linen-rag content. These are made in sheets varying from thin, 72-pound weight, to thick, 400-pound weight. These latter papers are so thick they do not have to be stretched before painting. Papers less than 140-pound weight must be stretched to prevent buckling when moistened.

Hot pressed (HP) papers are made with smooth, workable surfaces, while cold pressed (CP) papers come in a selection of smooth, coarse, and rough textures. You should try both HP and CP papers to understand fully the characteristics of each type.

Japanese rice papers are excellent for watercolor. These beautifully textured sheets provide a most responsive surface to both brush and paint. Nelson-Whitehead Paper Corp., 7 Laight Street, New York City, carries a large assortment of these exquisite papers.

There are non-woven fabric papers now on the market that simulate Japanese papers and are much less expensive. If you do not use too much water while painting, you might try working with these.

For certain "blotty" effects, unprinted newspaper pads are good. Newspaper is most absorbent and will drink in and deaden the color.

I recommend the following brands of watercolor paper: D'Arches, Fabriano, R.W.S. (Royal Watercolor Society).

Student watercolor papers are also available and are fairly good to use. Most of these must be moistened before painting but can be had in several textures and weights. Watercolor may also be used on illustration board and charcoal paper. Try these. See what happens!

Paint boxes

Purchase an enameled watercolor box that not only will store your tubes of color, but will also open into a palette and mixing area. This palette should be large

enough to contain at least 16 storage wells for fresh color. A box 4 1/2 x 12 inches is a convenient size to carry. Shop in the art supply store and examine several types of boxes before deciding on one. Always clean the mixing area of your paint box as soon as you have completed your painting.

Drawing boards

A pine drawing board or a piece of Masonite, 20 x 26 inches, is all you need to support your watercolor paper. For fastening the paper to the board, thumbtacks, staples and masking tape are good. Bulldog clips are not satisfactory. Remember, you won't be able to stick thumbtacks into the Masonite; use your tape.

Water containers

You will need a container to hold water for painting. Use a large container so that your colors will remain fresh and pure. Since you clean the brushes with water every time you change to a new color, the water quickly becomes gray and muddy. Gray water dulls the fresh paint. So change the water often!

Clean, empty No. 2 1/2 tin cans (no rusted ones, please) or quart-size glass jars make excellent water containers. You can find elaborate ones for sale in the art stores. Save your money and apply it to the purchase of good brushes.

Charcoal and pencil

You will want to make a preliminary sketch for your watercolor. Use a minimum amount of lines. A "B"

pencil or stick of medium-hard charcoal makes an excellent sketching tool. Erase all unnecessary marks before painting; otherwise these sketch lines will show through the watercolor. It is almost impossible to remove pencil or charcoal lines from wet paper, so complete all of your sketching while the paper is dry. As you acquire skill and confidence with the medium,

Erase all unnecessary lines

you will be able to paint directly with the brush with barely a preliminary sketch. Then your painting will become truly spontaneous!

Using rubber cement for resist

Erasers

Gum erasers will remove pencil marks and kneaded erasers are good for eliminating charcoal lines.

Rubber cement

One way to retain small areas of white, untouched paper is to cover these places with rubber cement, which will resist the overlayers of watercolor. When the cement dries, you can brush over it as you paint. When the painting is completed, the cement is rubbed off and the white areas will be revealed.

Finder

If you are painting out of doors and the subject matter is overwhelming and confusing, look through your finder. Move the finder around until you "frame in" what you wish to paint. A finder is simple to make. Take a 6 x 8 inch piece of cardboard and cut out an aperture 4 x 6 inches. That's all there is to it. Remember, "finder for focus." (See page 27.)

Stools

Most watercolorists like to paint while seated. For outdoor sketching, sit on a rock, a fence, or any comfortable spot. You could buy a collapsible stool of metal and fabric that is small and easy to carry.

Easels

I like to paint without an easel, holding the drawing board on my lap. This position, however, is sometimes inconvenient, as the paint can (and usually does) drip down onto your clothes. You can buy a collapsible easel on which you place the drawing board in a horizontal position. The paint drips if the board is held vertically. A word of advice! Some of the lightweight collapsible easels blow away in a strong gust of wind. If you use one of these, be sure to anchor it down with a couple of stones. Otherwise, your watercolor is apt to sail away while you are sketching out of doors. Using an easel also allows you complete freedom of both hands.

On a sketching trip in rural England, I found an enchanting village that I wanted to paint. Perched on a rock, I held the drawing board in my lap with one hand and used the other for manipulating my brush. As I painted, two kittens scampered out of a thatched-roof cottage and trampled through my open paint box that was lying on the ground. They sniffed me and proceeded to climb up my sleeve and over my shoulders smudging me with paint as they went. Since it had started to rain, I let the kittens have their way but continued to paint furiously, afraid that at any moment my watercolor would be washed out.

Fortunately a housewife living nearby discovered my predicament and came out to help me. She lifted the reluctant kittens from my shoulders and then graciously held an umbrella over me until I had finished the painting. My picture of her street seemed to have pleased her, because she invited me in for tea.

This was one time when not having an easel to work on proved an advantage. Had I been painting on one, my hands would have been free to take care of the kittens, but then I would have missed tea and crumpets in an English cottage.

Arranging the palette

Let's open the paint box and squeeze a generous amount of paint from the tubes onto the palette in

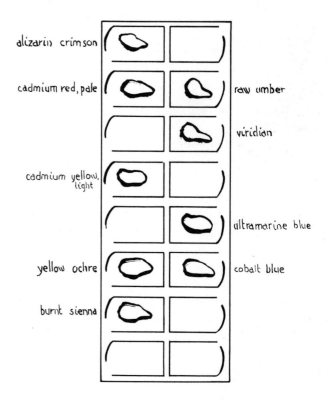

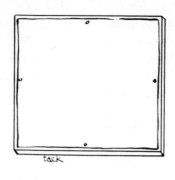

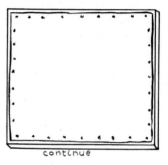

tack

smooth

continue

the following sequence (the colors in parenthesis can be added later):

alizarin crimson	(burnt umber)
cadmium red, light	raw umber
(cadmium orange)	viridian green
cadmium yellow, light	(thalo green)
(lemon yellow)	ultramarine blue
yellow ochre	cobalt blue
burnt sienna	(cerulean blue)
(raw sienna)	(ivory black)

You will notice the colors are arranged in order from red to blue, from warm to cool.

Since you ordinarily use up more of one color than another, you will soon be able to judge how much fresh paint to squeeze out of the tubes onto the palette. Be generous with the paint as you will need fully loaded brushes to paint in the spontaneous manner watercolor demands. If the paint is fresh and "juicy" your brush will load easily; otherwise, you have to rub it into the dried color. This may become frustrating when you are trying to work swiftly.

Preparing the watercolor paper

If you use heavy paper, fasten it directly to the drawing board. To achieve a uniform smoothness, first fasten down the center of each side of the paper. Then, smoothing as you go, put tacks or staples to the left and right of the centers until you reach the corners. Tacks or staples should be placed no more than two inches apart. The more fastenings you use, the less likelihood there will be of the paper buckling

wet

tape taut

Painting on crinkled paper

when wet. (You may prefer fastening the paper to the board with drafting tape.)

Paper less than 140-pound weight should be stretched before painting. To stretch the paper, wet it thoroughly on both sides with a loaded sponge and then lay it flat on your drawing board. Smooth the paper with your hand and sponge, making sure there are no wrinkles. This should be done while the paper is still wet. Then fasten the paper to your board. (Gummed paper tape, one inch wide, is a good binder for wet paper.) When the paper dries, it will be taut. Buckling will now be held to a minimum when you use your watercolors on the paper.

Crinkling the paper

Some artists have achieved interesting effects by painting on crinkled paper. To do this, select a thin watercolor paper and immerse it in water in the sink or in a flat cookie pan. After it is thoroughly wet, crinkle the paper, a small amount at a time, with your hands. As you crinkle, you will squeeze out excess water. Then lay the paper flat on the board and secure it. You can paint on the crinkled paper while it is still moist or wait until it has dried.

Now to paint

If you do not own an easel, put a couple of books under the back edge of the drawing board, allowing the front edge to rest on the table top. This will provide you with an inclined plane, which will permit the water to flow more readily. Your paints and brushes should be placed conveniently at your right for easy access. (I'm left handed, so I reverse this.)

THE WASH

Now that everything is ready and you are comfortable, let's try painting a wash. A wash is a smooth painted area all the same color or the same value. No white paper is visible and no brush strokes can be seen.

Do not paint over the wash to "even it up." To do so will cause streaking. Keep practicing until you have mastered this technique, trying various other colors and tones. To make the paint spread more easily, moisten your paper before you start the wash. Should you wish to paint a wash on wet paper, you will have to work most rapidly; you will also find that the wash will dry out much lighter than you had anticipated.

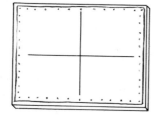

1. Divide the paper in halves, horizontally and vertically. This will provide four areas in which to practice.

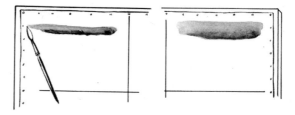

4. Run the brush horizontally across the top of the paper from left to right with a firm stroke.
5. You will notice that a narrow puddle has formed at the bottom of this painted line. Again working from left to right, paint through and below the puddle across the paper. The secret is to prevent the puddle from drying out by keeping the edge moist.

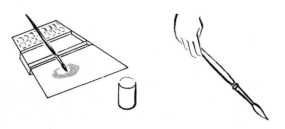

2. Using a generous amount of water, mix a quantity of color — let's say alizarin crimson — on your palette. Saturate the No. 9 or 1-inch sable brush with the color. Too much paint will cause the brush to drip.
3. Hold the brush near the end of the handle. This will allow a full arm movement and prevent you from wiggling the brush with your fingers.

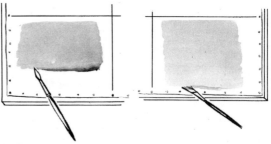

6. Repeat the horizontal strokes, moving the puddle lower and lower on the paper. If you run out of paint, recharge your brush.
7. When you reach the bottom of the paper and the puddle still remains, dry your brush and pick up the excess paint with it. Do not paint over the wash to "even it up." To do this will cause streaking.

THE GRADED WASH

To paint a graded wash (blending from dark to light) proceed as with a normal wash. Let's use blue paint this time.

Do not repaint an area, as you may pick up some color and cause blotching. Once the surface of the paper dries, overpainting will cause streaking. Keep practicing! Remember to clean your brush every time you change color.

3. To keep your graduation subtle, add only a little water with each stroke. To make the graduation more abrupt, simply use more water.

1. Start the first stroke with your brush fully charged with watercolor.

4. To lay a wash from light to dark, reverse the procedure. Start with your brush saturated with a light color. As you work down the paper keep adding more paint to the mixture with each stroke. At the bottom of the wash, pick up any excess paint with a dry brush or Kleenex.

2. As you work horizontally through the puddles, keep adding water to your paint mixture. The addition of water will cause the paint to lighten.

DRY BRUSH TECHNIQUE

Dry brush strokes are used to paint glittering water, or to show rough textures on trees, old barns, rocks or any "tortured" surface. By using a variety of brushes and textured papers you will discover an unlimited range of effects.

Dip your brush into the paint, using very little water. Now hold the brush at an angle to the paper or drag it on its side across the paper's surface. The slower the stroke, the drier the brush and the rougher the paper, the more texture you will obtain.

When being brushed, the paint adheres to the tiny peaks on the paper's surface leaving the hollows untouched and white.

Sometimes I like to vary my brush strokes by starting with the brush held straight. Then I gradually lower it on its side as it moves across the paper. If you apply a variety of pressures to the brush strokes, an interesting line emerges.

Using dry brush techniques, you may paint over colors and values and build up the textures to the quality you want.

Try painting dry brush strokes in many directions and shapes. Make the brush behave the way you want it to. Use the flat brush for large areas and your No. 3 red sable for delicate lines.

WET AND DRY TECHNIQUES

There are several methods in watercolor painting: wet, dry, or a combination of both.

The *wet* method calls for moistening or wetting the paper and laying on the color while the paper is still damp.

A moist paper provides a fine surface on which to work. It is excellent for painting skies, clouds, water, hills fading into the distance, or for getting soft, fuzzy edges. Fog, haze and rain are easy to depict on moist paper. Try blotting up the sky color with Kleenex to form clouds.

This wet method is not a good one for painting details!

As you work, you will begin to gauge the degree of wetness on which you enjoy painting.

If you have stretched your paper, or have fastened it securely to the board, you need not be concerned about buckling. However, every paper has its saturation point and if you use too much water the paper will turn into a mass of hills and valleys upon which it is impossible to paint. The heavier your watercolor paper, the more water it will tolerate.

Wet the paper by dipping it in water for a few minutes, or use a large brush or sponge saturated with water. Run the brush or sponge over the paper's surface starting at the top. Proceed in horizontal strokes from left to right making sure you do not skip any area. Continue with this process as though you were laying a wash. You can pick up excess moisture with a dry sponge or Kleenex.

I suggest you try this wet method on quarter-size sheets of paper. Use various weights and textures so that you can see what happens to the paper when it is thoroughly moistened.

Too-wet paper will soak up the paint. The paint will also run, making it difficult to control.

With the *dry* method, you will get crisp, clean lines and hard, sharp edges. The color is much easier to control, as the paper is dry and the only moisture is that provided by the watercolor itself. This dry technique is used for expressing strong sunlight and shadow, or glittering moonlight on the water. Rough textures on trees, weatherbeaten shacks or jagged rocks are naturals for this method of painting. If you enjoy working with detail, this technique is for you.

Many artists *mix* the wet and dry methods. For example, in painting a landscape, you might brush in the sky using the wet method and then paint in the foreground with the dry technique. After the sky has dried, or is almost dry, paint in the middle ground to achieve the mood you want.

You have undoubtedly discovered that when the paper is moist, a color creeps into its neighboring colors. This is due to capillary action. Some of the charm of watercolor is due to this phenomenon. Capitalize on it!

Sometimes when you have painted a watercolor on rough paper, hold it under the faucet in the sink and scrub off the color with a sponge or bristle brush. This procedure leaves a light stain of color on the paper. Allow the paper to dry for a bit, and, while it is still moist, paint over it with pure color and perhaps add some black India ink.

When you overwork a watercolor, it becomes muddy, tired and opaque. When this occurs, throw your paper into the wastebasket and start from scratch.

CORRECTIONS

You can "lift" areas of unwanted color or make corrections, even though I do not recommend this. You may like a painting except for one small error to be corrected. This correction may be done with a sponge, Kleenex, a bristle brush, a sharp knife or a razor blade. Moisten the areas before correcting. However, work dry if you use a knife or razor blade. Keep this face lifting process at a minimum!

INTENSIFYING

After completing your painting, you may want to intensify a certain area. Moisten the paper and then brush the desired color into place. A word of caution — the underlying color may mix with the new color and affect some of its brilliance.

OF ROCKS AND SEA by Mayo Sorgman.
Watercolor. Emily Lowe Award; Silvermine
Guild Award. (Photo: Nick Verderosa.)

ACCENTING

Now you may want to accent your painting with darks. Again, first moisten the area to be changed, and then paint in the darks you desire.

LINE AND FORM

You have demonstrated to yourself how to paint lines and shapes using the dry brush technique. Let's continue to paint lines with our other brushes and tools. It is amazing to find how many different types of lines you can paint with a given tool. Even an old "beat up" brush can be utilized. It will render an interesting rough, smudgy line.

As you have learned, lines vary according to the speed of the stroke and the wetness of the brush or paper. The pressure you exert also influences the width and strength of line. To prove the point, dip your No. 9 red sable brush in a generous amount of paint and try these:

1. Hold the brush erect and with as little pressure as possible paint a few thin lines.

2. Exert an increasing amount of pressure and paint successively thicker lines.

3. Now change the angle of the brush to the paper and dash off a few more lines. See how flexible the brush is and how many variations of lines you have painted.

You are now ready to paint something tangible. "In what direction shall I make the lines?" you might ask. Simply follow the basic structure of the object you wish to paint. Use horizontal strokes for the side of a barn, for a field, or low horizon or for water. Spherical objects, such as fruits, domes and archways, clouds, dishes, call for rounded strokes.

What kinds of lines would you use for a pine tree, marsh grass blowing in the wind, sand dunes, smoke, a pineapple?

MIXING COLOR

Now that you know how to make colors and values lighter by adding water, try experimenting with a specific color, say viridian, to see how many tints you can make. Or start with black and see if you can paint nine different values of gray before you reach paperwhite.

Making a tonal scale

Quickly draw nine small blocks across the top of the paper. Paint the fifth block a gray (black and water) that you think is halfway between black and white. Now fill in the remaining blocks with a sequence of grays that will make a good tonal scale. Should any of your blocks be darker or lighter? Can you adjust them? (See preceding page.)

I never mix black with my other colors to darken them, as black turns the colors drab. Black is excellent for accents or for outlines, should you want to use them.

As I have said, a rich black can be made by mixing alizarin crimson, burnt umber and ultramarine blue. You can also mix your own grays and make them warm or cool, light or dark. Make your own formulas. Start by mixing your complementary colors and take it from there.

Rich, deep purple can be made by mixing blues and reds. Each combination of the various blues and reds will give you a different purple.

As you know, red mixed with yellow produces orange and yellow mixed with blue makes green. However, for a truly bright orange, use your cadmium orange paint. For a vibrant green use the tube of viridian.

All of the watercolors can be freely mixed — two or three together. But — and this is a most important "but" — the more you mix, the grayer and drabber your colors become. To get sparkling, bright color in your painting, mix the colors *directly on the paper* instead of in the paint box. This takes courage but will add vibrancy to your color.

You can also put two colors on your brush at one time and watch them mix on the paper. Paint cadmium yellow over viridian green. Now try the viridian green over the cadmium yellow. Is there a difference? Use this "under and over" technique with other colors.

The amount of water you use will also have an effect on color mixing. Try using your pigment with very little water and then with much water. Any difference?

A good base for flesh tones is yellow ochre. Add a drop of cadmium yellow, or some burnt sienna or a bit of viridian to get your desired color. If you feel like painting a blue or a green face, however, go right ahead. You're the artist and it is your individual interpretation that is important.

You can make colors sing or moan, shout or whisper, sizzle or freeze.

Have you noticed that your colors seemed so much brighter when they were wet? — and as they dried, they became duller and lighter? Realizing this, *exaggerate your color* when painting. Make the reds redder, the blues bluer, the darks darker. Then, when your watercolor is dry, it will have the brilliance you originally intended.

WHAT COLORS FIRST?

In painting a watercolor you usually establish the darkest darks first. Since you know that your white will be the white of the paper, you are now able to plan the color range in composing the painting.

If you brush in the darks first, your watercolor will be dramatic and not dull. Then paint in the middle and light tones leaving as much white paper exposed as possible. This will give you a feeling of sunshine.

Watercolor calls for a bold, swift approach. Be direct — dash it off! If you don't succeed at first (and who does?) try another painting. Don't work over it laboriously. It has many times been said, that only one watercolor in fifty is really successful.

So much for the preliminaries. On with the main event! On the following pages I'll demonstrate a still life using the dry method, a landscape with the wet technique and a seascape with a combination of the two methods. Then you're on your own — the only way to become an artist!

Laying in the darks first

Matting and framing

You've painted a watercolor of which you are proud. Should you mat it, frame it, or do both?

I strongly recommend mats for all watercolors. The correct mat shows off a watercolor to its best advantage and accents its transparent quality. Over the mat goes the glass and a proper frame. I have never seen a painting, no matter how great, that has not been enhanced by good framing.

Now turn to the chapter "Framing Your Masterpiece" and learn what to do about your watercolor.

DRY TECHNIQUE Watercolor by Judy Martt, high school student. (*Scholastic Magazines*, New York.)

WET TECHNIQUE Watercolor by Jo Ann Loehrer, high school student. (*Scholastic Magazines*, New York.)

DRY TECHNIQUE

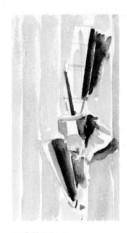

1. Darks first   *2.* Middle tones   *3.* Accents

WET TECHNIQUE

1. Darks first

3. Accents

2. Middle tones

1. Sketch

2. Darks

3. Middle tones

4. Accents

GOUACHE, EGG TEMPERA and casein have two characteristics in common — they are water soluble and opaque. In the previous chapter we learned about watercolor, which is also water soluble. What, then, are the main differences between these media?

To begin with, watercolor is transparent, while, as we have already noted, gouache, egg tempera and casein are not. When sufficiently thinned with water, however, these media also become transparent. And so we use them as both transparent and opaque media. In addition, due to its transparent quality, watercolor should not be painted over or it is apt to lose its characteristic brightness and become muddy. We may, however, and usually do, overpaint when using gouache, egg tempera and casein. In fact, gouache may be built up to a fairly thick impasto. To lighten watercolor, we merely add water; while to lighten gouache, egg tempera and casein, we *add white paint*.

We can use the same tools, painting surfaces and equipment for working with these water soluble media.

Materials and equipment

(Asterisks indicate basic equipment and colors. The other colors may be added after you have gained some skill with the media.)

Brushes
    *Red sable, round, Nos. 3 and 9
    *Red sable, 1 inch square end (flat)
    *Bristle brush, ⅛ inch
    House painter's brush, 2 inch (flat)

Other Painting Tools

*Rags	Toothpicks	*Knives
Twigs	Sponges	Razor blades
Brayers		

Gouache painting by David Noyes, high school student. (*Scholastic Magazines*, New York.)

TWELVE

Gouache, egg tempera and casein

Painting Surfaces

- *Illustration boards (double thick)
- *Watercolor papers (heavy, smooth and rough)
- Gesso panels
- Masonite panels
- Wood panels (for egg tempera)
- Canvas

Other Equipment

- *Drawing board, 20 x 26 inches (wood or Masonite)
- *Thumbtacks or staples with gun
- *Drafting tape, 1 inch wide
- *Paint box (old shoe box will do)
- Palette (shallow white enamel tray, 12 x 18 inches, flat cookie tin, or piece of plate glass)
- *Water container (quart glass jar)
- Medium charcoal and kneaded eraser
- *Pencils (B and H) and gum eraser
- Sharp pointed awl (for egg tempera)
- *Rags or Kleenex for absorbing excess water
- *Finder, 6 x 8 inches (make your own)
- Stool (portable)
- Easel (portable)
- Table or desk

Colors

RED	*Alizarin crimson
	Cadmium red, light
ORANGE	*Cadmium orange
YELLOW	*Cadmium yellow, light
	Lemon yellow
	*Yellow ochre
BROWN	*Burnt sienna
	Raw sienna
	*Burnt umber
	*Raw umber
GREEN	*Viridian
	Thalo green
BLUE	*Ultramarine blue
	Cobalt blue
	Thalo blue
BLACK	Ivory black
WHITE	Zinc white
	*Titanium white

Brushes

You can use the same brushes as those listed for painting watercolors. Refer to them on pages 80 and 82 to review their description and uses.

I am also adding a new brush for painting in gouache — an ⅛-inch bristle brush. You can use this for painting small areas of texture.

RED SABLE BRUSHES   Excellent for a smooth blending of paint, for making invisible strokes and for glazing. Use the No. 9 for large areas and the No. 3 for small areas and accents. Sable brushes hold a large quantity of paint and are a joy to use.

BRISTLE BRUSHES   Good for rough textures and thick strokes. Use these for building up a thick impasto. Bristle brushes are also good for scrubbing out unwanted areas. Too much scrubbing will make your painting "weary." It is much better to start fresh on a new painting. Keep your brushes clean. After use, be sure to wash them thoroughly in luke-warm soapy water and rinse. (Never use hot water.) With your fingers, squeeze out excess moisture, and lay the brushes flat. *Caution:* If you are using casein paint, make certain that you clean the brushes thoroughly before the paint dries on them. Otherwise you will have great difficulty in removing the dried paint. Dried casein will ruin your brushes!

Other painting tools

SPONGES AND RAGS   Use them for applying the preliminary layer of color on the ground or for painting areas of textured color. Each kind of sponge or rag provides you with a different surface texture.

HOUSE PAINTER'S BRUSH AND BRAYER   Wonderful for sweeping large areas of color in the preliminary stages of painting. Two or more colors can be applied by these tools at one time to create interesting effects.

TWIGS   Excellent for painting ragged, wiry lines, or for digging through thick paint to reveal the underpainting. Good for sgraffito.

TOOTHPICKS   Use these like twigs. Toothpicks, however, provide a much smoother, cleaner, more measured line than twigs. Also excellent for sgraffito.

KNIVES   For scraping off layers of paint, or for incising through the paint. They can also be used for applying paint to build up an impasto. But make sure you use *painting knives* for this. They are more flexible and will give you better results.

Painting surfaces

ILLUSTRATION BOARDS   Illustration boards are made of sheets of good quality white paper mounted on cardboard. They come in single, double and triple thicknesses and in rough and smooth surfaces. They are made particularly for work in watercolor, gouache, casein, egg tempera and ink. These boards come in sizes of 20 x 30 inches, 30 x 40 inches, and 38 x 60 inches. (Buy a large sheet and cut it into the sizes you want.) Illustration boards are used by both fine and commercial artists and provide excellent surfaces on which to work.

Recommended illustration boards:

Bainbridge No. 80
Bainbridge Sketch Board
Crescent Board
Strathmore Board

Visit your neighborhood art store and ask to examine some illustration boards.

Illustration boards are particularly good since they will not buckle when damp. However, if you work very wet, single thickness illustration boards will curl unless firmly attached to your drawing board. Double- or triple-thickness illustration boards do not have to be tacked to your drawing board, since they are firm enough to "stand on their own."

WATERCOLOR PAPER   Heavy, smooth watercolor papers are also good surfaces for painting with gouache, egg tempera and casein. These papers should be at least 140-pound weight. You understand that these watercolor papers must be securely fastened to your drawing board with thumbtacks, staples or drafting tape to prevent buckling when the paper becomes wet from the paint. (Refer to the watercolor section, pages 80 to 86.)

Recommended watercolor papers:

American Watercolor Society
D'Arches
Fabriano
Strathmore

Try several brands and decide which you like the best. You might also experiment with rough-textured papers to see what happens on coarse surfaces. Some interesting results might develop.

GESSO PANELS Many artists like to paint on gesso panels. These panels provide a firm surface on which to work. They are made of wood or Masonite and have been primed (covered) with gesso. (Gesso is a chalky paste that hardens like plaster of paris.) Some gesso panels come primed on both sides so that you can be economical and make two paintings on one board. (This may be fine for practicing, but if you made two good paintings, which side would you frame?) Gesso panels can be bought in sizes ranging from 8 x 10 inches to 24 x 36 inches. The Bocour Company manufactures good gesso panels.

Are you a "do-it-yourselfer"? Would you like to make your own gesso panels? Then, listen! At the lumber yard buy a panel of Masonite 4 x 4 feet. Have it cut into a number of sizes you find convenient to work on. (See below.)

1. At home, paint *both* sides of each panel with a thin glue solution. Allow these panels to dry thoroughly.

2. Now paint each side with *three* coats of gesso.

Let it dry thoroughly between each coat. (You can buy gesso — Bocour Artist Colors — in pint or quart containers ready mixed, or you can purchase a dry gesso compound and mix it yourself.)

3. After the final coat has dried, rub it with a very fine sandpaper.

4. & 5. And this is your gesso panel. One side will be smooth and the other will be textured. Try painting on both surfaces and find out if it makes any difference to your painting.

MASONITE PANELS Another good painting surface is the Masonite panel. To prepare Masonite for painting, give it three thin coats of white casein paint, allowing each coat to dry before applying the next. You will find that the rough side of the Masonite is much more absorbent than the smooth side. If you prefer to paint on this textured side, I suggest you give it two extra coats of the white casein paint.

PREPARING THE GROUND After you have prepared the Masonite panels, paint one with a light yellow-ochre casein, one with light blue, and one with light green casein. Let them dry. Now make a painting using each of these tinted grounds. Do you prefer this

1

2

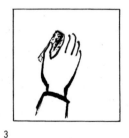

3

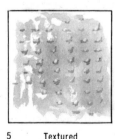

4   Smooth

5   Textured

to working on a white surface? Does it set the "tone" of your painting? Does it suggest a "jumping-off" point for color schemes?

If you enjoy working on tinted grounds, you might pre-color your illustration boards or watercolor papers. Make sure that the working surfaces are completely dry before you begin painting. Otherwise, you may regretably find that the color will pick up and mix with the paint you later apply. But you will learn by doing!

CANVAS   I would like to add this one additional painting surface to your list. (See the discussion of canvas on page 57.) A casein painting on canvas is very difficult to distinguish from an oil painting. Textured canvas makes a fascinating surface for gouaches.

Palette

A piece of window or plate glass about 12 x 18 inches makes a fine palette particularly if you do not have an enameled tray or a cookie tin to spare, and the glass is easier to clean! Since gouache, egg tempera and casein paint are not used as thin as watercolor, you need not be concerned with "runny" paint on the glass palette. Use casein of about the consistency of cream as you do with gouache and egg tempera.

Gouache – with gusto

What gouache really is

All paintings made with an opaque watercolor (such as egg tempera, poster colors, casein) are often called gouaches. True gouache, however, is a distinct water-soluble paint which is made opaque by the addition of finely powdered clay to the pigment.

Like watercolor, gouache is a spontaneous medium which can be dashed off with verve and gusto. It is at its best when it is used as *both* a transparent and opaque medium. It dries quickly and can be freely overpainted. It may also be underpainted and glazed or built up to a fairly thick impasto. Too thick an application of paint may cause later cracking. As you work you will learn how heavy an impasto can be used safely. Like watercolor, gouache dries out lighter when finished and has a dull (mat) surface.

When working with watercolor, you add water to the paint in order to make a color lighter. But with gouache, you add *opaque white* to the color to make

CHICAGO STREET IN WINTER by Aaron Bohrod. Gouache, 1939. (*Whitney Museum of American Art,* New York.)

lighter tints. Gouache does not have the brilliance or sparkle of watercolor, since the white paper does not glisten through the opaque paint as it does with the transparent watercolor.

Gouache lends itself to unusual methods of painting. While we shall give you only basic techniques, gouache is a medium where "anything goes." Gouache can convey the feeling of a watercolor or an oil painting, or it can combine the characteristics of both. It truly is a most versatile medium, easy to use and allowing full opportunity for individual creative expression.

The important thing to remember about gouache is its paint quality — a combination of both transparent and opaque areas within a single painting.

A bit of the past

Artists have always used an opaque paint that was water soluble. They cooked roots, berries, vegetables and tree bark to get color. Then, in order to give the paint body, they added gypsum or chalk. Boiled animal skins provided the necessary adhesive for the paint.

During the Renaissance, gouaches were usually made as preliminary sketches for oil paintings. In the nineteenth century gouaches were beginning to be recognized as works of art in their own right. Toulouse-Lautrec, Rouault, and other modern French painters developed gouache painting to a high degree.

Today's artists are fond of gouache. Some of the best known American painters working in this medium are Adolf Dehn, Aaron Bohrod, Arnold Blanch, Doris Lee, Martyl, Mark Tobey, Morris Graves and the late Yasuo Kuniyoshi.

Gouache paints

Gouache is bought in tubes. It is manufactured by a number of companies including Winsor and Newton, Grumbacher, and Talens.

The list of colors I have given you (page 104) comprises a basic set with which you can achieve almost any effect that you want. You may add to this roster of colors as you acquire experience. The colors with the asterisks are "musts." Your color selection will mirror your individuality. However, a "word to the wise" — keep your color schemes simple and harmonious. Too many colors make harsh, unpleasant paintings. You will notice that great artists use comparatively few colors in their works.

Since you will use a large quantity of white when painting in gouache, buy large tubes. Otherwise you will find that your supply of white will be quickly exhausted. Always use fresh paint. This may sound extravagant, but your painting will go much easier if your paint is fresh, juicy and flowing.

In order to assure fresh *moist* paint, keep the tube caps securely screwed so that the paint cannot dry out. If the caps have stuck, run warm water over them — and, presto, they will open.

Gouache materials and equipment. (Photo: Nick Verderosa.)

Arranging the palette

Let's distribute the paint on the palette in order from white to blue and from warm to cool — just as you did with watercolors.

Since you use much more white than any other color, remember this when setting up your palette — lots of white! After you have painted a few gouaches you will have a good idea as to how great a quantity of each color to set out.

Arrange the colors around the outside of your palette using the center as a mixing area (and keep the palette clean).

Techniques

COLOR MIXING

All of your colors can be intermixed.

As I have said, to make the colors lighter, add opaque white. To make your colors darker, simply add a darker color or black. Black should be used sparingly, as it has a tendency to "gray off" the colors and kill their brilliance. I like to reserve black for accents only. Using too much white, on the other hand, will give your gouache a chalky appearance. You will learn by experimenting.

For the utmost brilliance, use colors right out of the tubes. The more you mix, the duller the colors become. Try to mix the colors directly on the painting itself rather than on your palette. Color mixed in this manner has more vibrancy and bounce.

Have plenty of paint on hand. Gouache handles best when it is the consistency of light cream. This provides easy control of the medium and prevents running.

Use water to thin your paints. If you have used too much water in the painting, simply blot up the excess with Kleenex or an absorbent rag. Remember: too much water will cause your paper to buckle. Watch it!

Shall we mix a few colors to get used to the gouache medium? How about these:

Try painting a ladder. The bottom rung is black. As you climb the ladder the rungs become progressively lighter until they are white at the top.

You have discovered a new plant. It has fifteen leaves — each of which is a different green ranging from yellow-green to blue-green.

There are a few bananas in the fruit bowl. Some are not ripe, one is pure yellow, and the others are over-ripe. How do you mix the browns? Now experiment with mixing blue and orange, red and green, purple and yellow, etc. Let's add some grapes to the bowl. These grapes are bluish, or reddish or purplish. Now add raspberries, limes and plums.

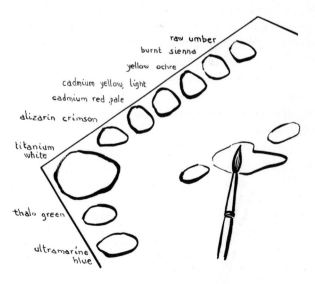

Mix orange and red. Start with orange and add red to it. Now reverse the procedure. Any difference? Try this first with thick paint and then with water-thinned paint. Are the results the same?

How many different kinds of gray can you make? Are there more left to discover?

To insure pure color, there are two **MUSTS**:

1. Clean your brush every time you change color.

2. Change the water as soon as it becomes muddy; muddy water makes muddy paint!

INTENSIFYING

If you wish to make a color brighter, you may either wait until it has dried and then paint over it with the intensity you want, or scrub the color out with your bristle brush and repaint. Do this latter with care so that you do not disturb too much of the painting's surface.

THE WASH

We are going to paint a clear blue June sky. Fasten a piece of heavy 9 x 12 watercolor paper to your board. Divide this into quarters so that you can easily estimate the amount of paint to use. Have your No. 9 red sable brush ready, your palette set out with color, a container of water and a rag. After you have done this exercise, paint the remaining three areas of your paper. Keep practicing until you can paint a good wash.

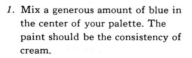

1. Mix a generous amount of blue in the center of your palette. The paint should be the consistency of cream.

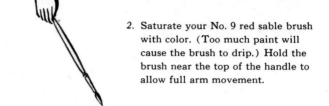

2. Saturate your No. 9 red sable brush with color. (Too much paint will cause the brush to drip.) Hold the brush near the top of the handle to allow full arm movement.

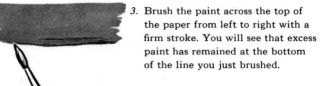

3. Brush the paint across the top of the paper from left to right with a firm stroke. You will see that excess paint has remained at the bottom of the line you just brushed.

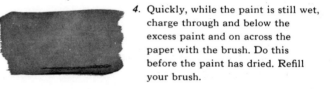

4. Quickly, while the paint is still wet, charge through and below the excess paint and on across the paper with the brush. Do this before the paint has dried. Refill your brush.

5. Keep repeating the horizontal strokes from left to right, always painting over the bottom of the preceding stroke. Recharge your brush as needed. Pick up excess paint at the bottom with a dry brush.

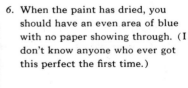

6. When the paint has dried, you should have an even area of blue with no paper showing through. (I don't know anyone who ever got this perfect the first time.)

THE GRADED WASH

This time you will paint a glorious sunset sky that ranges from dark to light. Choose your own color. Mix a good quantity of it in the center of the palette and make certain that a generous amount of white paint is available. Everything ready?

1. Proceed as with a normal wash.

2. Start your first stroke with the brush fully charged with color.

3. As you work horizontally, add *white* to the brush each time it needs more paint.

4. Do not repaint to "even it up."

5. Pick up excess paint on the bottom with a dry brush.

6. When it is dry, you should have a nicely graded sky.

This was a bit more difficult to do, wasn't it? Practice with other graded skies until you are proficient in painting them. How about painting a graded wash from light to dark? Just reverse the above procedure. Start with a light color and keep adding darker color as you work horizontally down the paper.

Now try a wash blending from one color to another. This is tricky, but I'm sure you can do it.

DRY BRUSH TECHNIQUE

Interesting textures can be obtained by using a dry-brush technique. It is as its name implies — dry brush.

Simply charge your brush with very little paint and no water. Drag the brush (or any other painting tool) over the area to be covered. The dry brush will leave a ragged, broken line of color. The amount of color can be regulated by your pressure on the brush. The heavier the stroke, the more paint will be deposited. Experiment with this dry-brush technique using a variety of brushes, twigs, sponges, etc., and discover the many fascinating textures that can be produced.

WET AND DRY TECHNIQUES

As we have said previously, gouache is a versatile medium and allows for a complete range of techniques. You may use the paint wet, thin and flowing, as in watercolor, or dry and thick, as in oil. You may also use a combination of the wet and dry techniques

Gouache painting by Dennis Lund, high school student.
(*Scholastic Magazines*, New York.)

in one painting. It is this combination of the wet and dry — thick and thin impasto — that gives gouache its distinctive style.

The wet technique lends itself to clouds and water, and all soft, fuzzy edges. The dry technique is used for firm, positive strokes, for clean hard lines and sharp edges.

Paint a simple landscape using thin gouache. Paint the same landscape again using comparatively thick paint. Now, repaint it once more, this time using a combination of the two techniques, building up some areas of the painting with an impasto. It is this third method that is recognized as typical gouache painting.

UNDERPAINTING

Some artists like to sketch a complete composition first with neutral colors and then, when this has dried, repaint it with other colors to build up and complete the painting.

This first application of color is called *under-painting*, which we discussed in Chapter 10. The colors to use for your underpainting are determined by the overall tone you want your completed painting to be. If it is to have a warm, sunny feeling, the underpainting might be done with yellow ochres, oranges or dull reds. Should you want the painting to be dominated by a cool glow, then underpaint in blues or greens. Avoid strong contrasts of light and dark. Make your sketch flat — like a poster!

Almost any color but black may be used for underpainting. Make a pencil sketch of a simple still-life and repeat this five or six times on a sheet of paper. Now underpaint each of these sketches with a different color — some warm and some cool. After these are thoroughly dry, paint over each of them using the same color scheme. Did they all look alike when you finished? What, if any, were the differences? Did the underpainting glow through the added colors?

You will find that the underpainting colors will sometimes mix with the overpainting and come through in an opaque manner.

OVERPAINTING

Suppose you have painted a gouache, but you do not like several passages of color. What to do? Simple. Overpaint it!

If your original color is thoroughly dry, you may overpaint as many as five or six times — if you are careful. If the original color is not dry, it will "bleed" through and mix with each successive coat of paint. There may be times when this is desirable — or disastrous — depending upon what you want for a final effect. Often when painting, accidental effects turn out advantageously and open up new paths to pursue. Be on the alert and make the most of each turn of events.

When you overpaint, you may build up a thick impasto wherever you wish. Then, with your knife, toothpick, or the wooden end of your brush, scratch through this impasto while it is still wet and allow the underpainting to show through. You can arrive at some charming and interesting results in this manner.

Are you ready for another experiment? Get out your supplies and materials. We'll do this on a prepared piece of Masonite.

1. Paint a thin wash of yellow-ochre on the white Masonite.

2. Let it dry.

3. Using various values of orange, underpaint an autumn scene with a country road, a barn and old trees. Make no attempt at light and shade but paint flat areas. Paint freely with large strokes.

4. Now let this dry.

5. Next, overpaint it with local color — the sky, the red barn, the country road, the fall foliage.

6. Brush in the sky with thin paint. Accent the old barn and a few trees in the foreground with a thick impasto.

7. Complete the painting as you wish.

8. You have just painted a characteristic gouache.

To explore another intriguing technique, repaint the autumn scene. After you have finished, wash over the entire painting with water. While it is still wet, work other colors into the surface. You will get floating color and soft edges with this technique.

GLAZING

A glaze, as we have already learned, is simply a transparent thin coat or wash of color. Now, let's experiment.

1. Paint a red apple.

2. When this has thoroughly dried, paint over it with a thin wash of alizarin crimson.

3. Let this dry.
4. Now cover it with another wash of alizarin.
5. Wait until this has dried thoroughly.
6. Repaint with a third wash of alizarin.

You will notice that each layer of red glaze contributed a further glow to the apple.

You can glaze either a small section or an entire painting or "warm" or "cool" a painting with the proper glaze. You may change the color of an object by glazing it with another color. Try exploring with glazes. You will need patience in waiting for your color to dry between each application, but it is worth it.

It is possible the glaze might pick up some of the color underneath and cause exciting effects.

ADDING OTHER MEDIA

Gouache may be combined successfully with pastel, pen and ink, oil or pencil. You might underpaint or overpaint with these media and then compare the results.

SIMULATING WATERCOLOR OR OIL

Gouache, as you have found, has unlimited possibilities. You can paint it wet and thin and have it look like a watercolor or you can paint it opaque with an impasto and make it resemble an oil painting.

To make your gouache further resemble an oil, let it dry; then give it one or two coats of varnish. Make sure that the first application of varnish has completely dried before you give it its second or final coat. You may object to the shiny finish caused by the varnish. If you do, you can eliminate the shine by rubbing a very thin white wax over the surface.

What to paint first

There are two things I should like to impress upon you:

1. Always paint large areas first.

2. Start painting with a large brush and finish with a small brush for details and accents.

It is usually best to paint skies and foregrounds first and then develop them as you work. It is much easier to paint a house or a tree over the sky than it is to paint the sky around a tree or building. After the sky and the foreground have been quickly painted in with large brushes, freely establish the darkest areas, then the medium, and finally the lightest areas. The surface is now completely covered. From now on, work back and forth over the painting keeping all of the parts "alive" as you progress.

If you work on a tinted surface, such as green or red, you will find that it establishes the medium tone of the painting. You then freely paint in the dark areas and add the light ones. Keep the values of your painting simple — light, medium and dark. Do not use too many in-between tones because too great a value range may rob your painting of its unity and strength.

Matting and framing

"Shall I mat my gouache or just put a frame around it?" This is a question often asked of me.

The decision is yours to make. If you want the painting to have a light feeling, then mat it like a watercolor. If your gouache is turbulent with thick impasto, however, then frame it like an oil — with no mat.

Read the chapter "Framing your Masterpiece" for further information.

Painting a landscape

I shall now demonstrate for you painting a landscape in gouache. This is the method I use, but it is certainly not the only way to paint in this medium. Another method may be better for you. However, you can always learn something by watching others perform. So here goes!

1. Sketch

2. Darks

3. Medium tones

4. Final details

Egg tempera – a perennial favorite

Are you interested in painting for posterity and having your masterpiece last for a thousand years? Then use egg tempera — one of the most permanent of all painting media. In museums you can see rich glowing egg tempera paintings on wooden panels done by Italian artists in the thirteenth and fourteenth centuries. Despite their great age, these tempera panels have weathered time and are in an excellent state of preservation.

Going back

Egg tempera painting, like gouache, was known and practiced by the Egyptians, Greeks and Romans. Byzantine altarpieces were often done in egg tempera. In the fourteenth century, Giotto, one of the greatest artists of the early Renaissance, used egg tempera. Because of the nature of the medium, these paintings were rather small and were executed on wood or gesso panels. Tempera as an art medium was popular with Italian and Flemish painters until the time of the Van Eyck brothers, about 1400, when the oil technique was invented.

MADONNA AND CHILD by a follower of Duccio. Egg tempera, early XIV century. (*The Metropolitan Museum of Art,* New York, Marquand Fund, 1920.)

BIRD IN THE SPIRIT by Morris Graves. Egg tempera, c. 1940-41. (*Whitney Museum of American Art,* New York, gift of the Friends of the Whitney Museum of American Art.)

The paint itself

Just what is egg tempera? It is a dry pigment mixed with an emulsion of egg yolk and water. The name comes from the Italian *tempera* — a liquid used as a binder for pigment.

Egg tempera, like gouache and casein, is water soluble. In addition, it may be mixed with oil and used as an oil paint. Like the other water soluble paints, tempera dries out lighter and has a mat finish. It may be (and usually is) underpainted, overpainted or glazed (see pages 112-113). With the advent of oil painting, egg tempera lost its appeal as an art medium. It was not until the late nineteenth century that its painterly qualities were rediscovered and artists again began to use this medium.

Egg tempera today

Andrew Wyeth, one of America's best known contemporary artists, paints with egg tempera. He is a meticulous craftsman and uses the medium in the slow, methodical manner of traditional tempera painters. Mark Tobey of the West Coast is also an enthusiastic practitioner of the medium. Other Magic Realist painters, like Trew Hooker, use tempera because of its luminosity and its unique facility for painting in great detail.

More about the medium

Instead of being purely opaque, egg tempera has a semi-opaque, translucent quality that causes any underpainting to glow luminously. Whereas watercolor and gouache can be used with great freedom, tempera

RECONSTRUCTION by Ben Shahn. Egg tempera, 1945. (*Whitney Museum of American Art,* New York.)

calls for a slow, planned approach. The traditional egg tempera painting is done with small red sable brushes and each thin brush stroke is visible. The brush strokes are cross hatched, layer on layer, to build up form. Even the large areas are painted with small brush strokes.

Usually the composition is painstakingly sketched in great detail with pencil and then sprayed with fixative, or scratched into a gesso or wooden panel with an awl. Then it is carefully underpainted. When the underpainting is dry, overpainting or glazing begins and continues until the picture is completed. Fortunately, tempera dries almost immediately so that you can paint over it with ease.

If you work in the traditional manner (and you don't have to), the surface of the egg tempera painting is kept smooth without any impasto build up. The painting is built very carefully in thin layers. (I find tempera painting too restrictive for my temperament. My personal favorite is watercolor.)

If properly executed, an egg tempera painting will neither yellow nor crack with age. But if the paint is applied too heavily, it will flake off when dry.

Although tempera dries with a mat finish, you can make the painting glow if you rub it with a soft cloth when it is dry. This will impart a very pleasant sheen.

To make a tempera painting resemble an oil painting, just give it a coat or two of damar varnish. Remember, the painting must be dry before the varnish is applied, and thoroughly dry between each coat of varnish.

Egg tempera paint

Some egg tempera paints are packaged in tubes like oil paints and are easy to squeeze out. You can also buy dry color pigment and mix it with an emulsion of egg yolk to make your own brand of tempera. At this time, however, I would not advise this. Do not confuse the tempera poster paints or showcard colors you used in school with the egg tempera paints that I recommend.

Two good prepared tempera paints:

1. *Martin Tempera Colors* manufactured by the Nobema Products Corp. and made of pure pigment in an egg oil and gum emulsion.

2. *Rowney Egg Tempera Colors* produced by the Morilla Co., Inc., and prepared with pure pigment and fresh egg yolk.

Brushes

If you use egg tempera in the traditional manner, you may limit your brushes to the four listed. The flat sable can be used for underpainting, the No. 3 and No. 9 for the overpainting, and the bristle brush for scrubbing out any unwanted color.

If you do not wish to follow the traditional manner of painting with tempera, however, you may be adventurous and use any painting tools you wish. Experiment with a number of painting tools and brushes. Find out how the results differ from those you obtain with the red sable brushes. Red sable brushes hold a good amount of paint. In addition, they retain their

Egg tempera materials and equipment. (Photo: Nick Verderosa.)

shape and are wonderful for painting fine, firm lines. A good red sable brush is indispensable. It is very responsive and sensitive to the touch. As usual, change from large brushes to the smaller ones as your work progresses.

Painting surfaces

For satisfactory results use gesso or Masonite panels as painting surfaces for your paintings. You can buy prepared panels in the art stores or make your own. Refer to the section on surfaces for information on the preparation of gesso and Masonite panels (pages 106-107). You may use either white or tinted grounds. (Good wood panels are expensive, so we'll do without them for now.)

Heavy, smooth watercolor paper and double-thick illustration board are also used as grounds for painting with tempera. But make sure the paper is securely fastened to the drawing board before you begin to paint; otherwise, it may buckle when moistened.

If you are planning to work on a gesso panel, you may find it exciting to incise your drawing into the surface with a sharp-pointed awl. Many of the Old Masters used this technique.

You will find it much simpler, however, to use a pencil. A long pointed "H" pencil is good for this purpose. It is advisable to make the drawing first, in great detail, on a piece of tracing paper and then transfer it onto your ground with the "H" pencil.

Palette

Choose either a shallow enameled pan, a cookie tin or a sheet of glass about 12 x 16 inches.

Squeeze the colors from the tubes around the outside of the palette in the same sequence you used for watercolor and gouache.

Caution! Deposit only as much color on your palette as you will need at one time, as dried out tempera paint is not easy to use. You can keep the paint moist longer by adding a few drops of water to each color as you squeeze it onto your palette. Keep the center of the palette clear for mixing.

After you have completed your day's work, clean the entire palette with soapy water and a rag. Rinse and dry it thoroughly. Do not leave any paint on your palette overnight.

Techniques

CONTROL OF THE PAINT

Egg tempera should be used the consistency of milk. It should flow freely from your brush but should neither "drag" nor be uncontrollably thin. You will soon learn what consistency will be best for your individual technique. Always work from light to dark.

When using tempera, it is convenient to use a flat table. Prop a few books under the panel or drawing board to create a low angle. This facilitates a smooth flow of paint without being steep enough to cause the paint to run.

MIXING

Egg tempera colors may be safely intermixed with one another. To make a color lighter, add white or a color lighter than the one you are using. To darken a color, simply add a darker color. Here again, as with other water-soluble media, I do not recommend mixing black with your colors, as black imparts a tired, gray quality. Colors may be warmed or cooled, grayed or intensified by the proper mixing. Refer to the chapter on color to refresh your memory!

PAINTING A SMOOTH AREA

Even if we want to have each brush stroke show, can we paint a smooth area? Of course!

Divide a sheet of illustration board into several rectangles, 4 x 6 inches. Now mix a quantity of a color, say green, in the middle of your palette.

Using your No. 9 red sable brush, paint a horizontal line clear across the top of the first rectangle. Paint another brush stroke of green immediately below this in the same direction — from left to right. Now paint another line below this, and another and another until you reach the bottom of the rectangle. Refill your brush as needed. You have noticed that each brush stroke has dried before you painted one

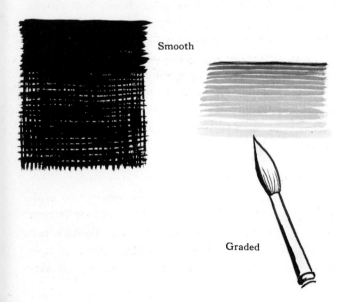

Smooth

Graded

below it. This is the nature of egg tempera! You did not work in large sweeping areas as you did with watercolor or gouache. Your method was a slow, line-by-line technique. If you left any white paper showing through, paint over these areas with horizontal brush strokes. Cross-hatch the horizontal lines with vertical strokes. You now have a smooth area.

PAINTING A GRADED AREA

A graded area is a bit more difficult to paint, but it is a challenge. This time we'll use red. Squeeze a generous amount of red in the center of your palette and, near it, a quantity of white.

1. Dip the red sable brush into red paint and brush a line across the top of the second rectangle.

2. Paint another line directly under this.

3. As you recharge your brush, add a bit of white paint to the red.

4. If the paint begins to thicken, add a few drops of water to keep it flowing smoothly.

5. Continue down the paper, adding more and more white to the red paint with each horizontal stroke.

6. You now have painted a graded area.

In the other rectangles, try blending a graded area from:

> dark red to pink,
> yellow to orange,
> purple to blue,
> white to black.

Make certain that each brush stroke is revealed!

Is it easier to paint from light to dark or from dark to light? Do you enjoy this line-by-line method of painting?

CONTOUR PAINTING

When using tempera, the best results in modeling and shading are produced by making your brush strokes follow the contour of the object you are painting. By doing this, the brush strokes will seem to "grow" from the object.

Try an apple, a pear, a glass, a bottle, a rock, a series of waves. The strokes may be horizontal or vertical in direction and may also be cross-hatched.

Now paint an old piece of driftwood, a branch of pussywillows, a cobble-stone street, an egg.

DRY BRUSH

The dry-brush technique in tempera is the same as that used with other media. Just drag a brush with little paint and no water over an area to create texture.

UNDERPAINTING AND OVERPAINTING

If you want to underpaint, thin the tempera with water and apply it as a wash with the wide, flat, red sable brush. Light colors are best for underpainting and can be used to set the mood of the picture. Burnt sienna makes an excellent underpainting for flesh tones. You may either underpaint in flat tones or carefully model the objects with light and shade. You can then overpaint layer on layer and build up your painting putting darker colors over lighter ones. Continue the line technique and cross-hatch as you work.

GLAZING

Glazing may also be practiced when working with tempera. As you recall, a glaze is a transparent layer of paint darker than the one on which it is applied. You can glaze a painting to warm or cool an area or to change a specific color. After glazing, you can con-tinue to paint with the traditional line technique and, if you wish, do more glazing.

SCUMBLING

Scumbling, as you have already read, is painting a lighter color over a darker one. This technique calls for a thicker paint than the rest of your painting. I would suggest you scumble as little as possible when painting with tempera, particularly if you want to retain the *smooth* surface so characteristic of the medium.

Contour painting

Dry-brush

ADDING OTHER MEDIA

Ink and oil paint may be combined with egg tempera to create interesting results. Many of the early oil paintings were combinations of tempera and oil. The underpainting was done in tempera and then over-painted with oil.

CORRECTING

To eliminate an unwanted color or to change an area in a painting, you may carefully scratch it out with a sharp razor blade. Or you can scrub it out with a moist bristle brush and then repaint. Either technique is difficult. If you find yourself making too many corrections it is best to throw the painting away and start anew.

Varnishing

Egg tempera paintings may be glossed with damar varnish. When varnished, temperas are almost indistinguishable from oils. (One or two coats of varnish is sufficient.)

Matting and framing

"To mat or not to mat," that is the question. If your tempera painting is light and gay, treat it like a watercolor and mat it. Otherwise, simply put it in a suitable frame — as you would an oil painting.

I shall now demonstrate painting a still life using the traditional technique. Notice the contour drawing and the line treatment — particularly in the drapery.

1. Sketch

2. Spray

3. Underpaint

4. Overpaint and glaze

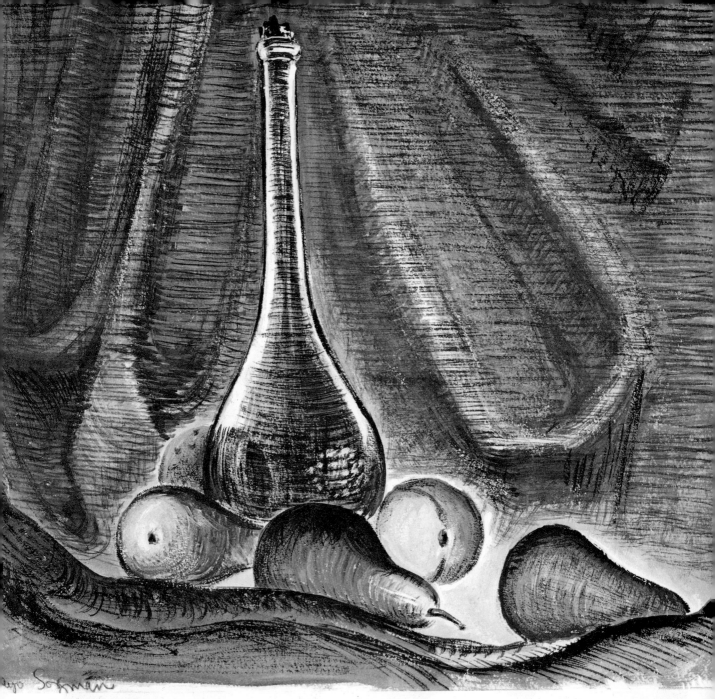

5. Finished painting

Casein – the versatile medium

Casein is a medium closely resembling oil. You'll enjoy working with it.

For both oil and casein painting, you can use the same painting surfaces, the same brushes and tools and the same techniques. In fact, a casein painting can actually look like an oil. What then is the difference between oil and casein?

Casein is water soluble and oil is not. While casein dries quickly, oil is slow drying. Casein is excellent for outdoor sketching as there are no wet canvases to worry about when you are ready to pack up and leave. Casein is clean to use and oil is apt to be messy. (Soap and water dissolve casein while oil requires turpentine.) And, of course, the basic paints are chemically different. Casein is really a protein glue made from skimmed milk. When properly mixed with color pigments, it becomes casein paint. Casein paint is opaque.

How it came about

Casein is a medium that was used by the early Egyptians for decorating walls with paintings and hieroglyphics. It was also used by the early Hebrews and the artists of Greece and Rome. Because of its excel-

THE LABYRINTH by Robert Vickrey. Casein, 1951. (*Whitney Museum of American Art*, New York.)

lent adhesive quality, casein was a popular painting medium. And being water soluble, it was easy to handle. It could also be painted over when dry.

Casein was used for easel paintings until the fifteenth century, when oil paint was discovered. Michelangelo and other Renaissance artists used casein both for finished paintings and for underpainting oils. Casein survived as a painting medium throughout the centuries. Often artists used it for making sketches. Then, in the 1800's, artists again began to use casein for finished works. Ever since, casein painting has risen in popularity. Today, because of its versatility, casein is used widely. A few well-known American artists who work in casein with great success are Anton Refregier, Aaron Bohrod, Ben Shahn, Julian Levi, Stuart Edie and Morris Graves. Look for their works at exhibits and when you visit museums.

Materials and equipment

You can use the same painting surfaces and equipment that you purchased for egg tempera and gouache. (Try painting with casein on canvas.) Refer to the lists on pages 103-107.

Casein paint

Casein paints are permanent and will not fade. The colors may be intermixed as you wish. But, as in watercolor, the more you mix, the duller and grayer your colors become. Try to use as much pure color as possible.

To mix a lighter color, add white. To make the color darker, add a darker color of your choice.

For easier brushing, you may want to thin the casein paint with water. But if you are working with a palette knife, use the paint thick.

When dry, casein paint has a dull, mat finish. If varnished, it becomes glossy.

Because of the powerful adhesive quality of casein, it is very important to clean your brushes thoroughly with soap and lukewarm water after using them and before they dry out; otherwise the paint will cake and the brushes will be ruined — and you'll need another allowance for more brushes! Casein dries much quicker than you think; so be on the alert! It is also wise to clean your brush when changing from one color to another. This simple precaution will assure you of fresh, clear color.

I have constantly told you to be liberal with your paint and to put generous amounts of it on your palette. But now I am taking back this advice. Place on your palette only the amount of casein you will be using for an hour! When exposed to the air, casein hardens quickly and solidly. You might try adding a few drops of water to the fresh paint to prevent it from drying out too quickly.

There are several superior brands of casein paint on the market. I have been pleased with both Shiva Original Casein Colors and Permanent Pigments "V" Casein Colors. These paints are packaged in standard studio-size tubes, 1 x 4 inches, and come in a variety of colors. Talens "Eta" Casein colors also have an extensive color selection but are packaged in 2-ounce jars. (Keep the caps or lids of the casein tubes and jars tightly closed so that the paint will not dry out.)

Color

The list of colors on page 104 is a good one to con-

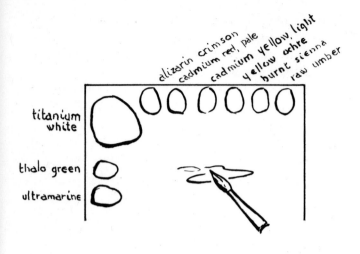

alizarin crimson
cadmium red, pale
cadmium yellow, light
yellow ochre
burnt sienna
raw umber

titanium white

thalo green

ultramarine

tinue with. Retain the same sequence in setting up your palette. Then, when you paint, you will automatically know where your colors are. Have fun with color and see how many hues you can make! Try mixing three colors together; or two warm colors; a cool and a warm color. What happens when you mix a color with black? Can you discover how to mix a bright orange or a clear, vibrant green?

Mix casein to match the color of your skin, your eyes, your hair, your clothing — a penny, a quarter, your gold ring, the tree bark outside your window.

Easy? I wonder.

Techniques

The typical casein painting has a smooth surface with little, if any, impasto. Usually it is painted with red sable brushes so that the brush strokes are blended and barely visible. As a creative artist, however, you need not be restricted by painting casein in this man-

ner. Any kind of brush or tool may be used to obtain the effects and surface textures that you want. Refer to the section on gouache painting. Reread the methods used to obtain smooth and graded areas of color. Now practice these same techniques with casein.

Casein, too, may be underpainted, overpainted, glazed and scumbled. (See pages 112-114.) Just remember that a glaze is a *thin, transparent* coat of color darker than the color over which it is applied. Scumbling is the method of applying an *opaque, lighter* color over a darker one. Very often, interesting results are obtained by allowing some of the darker color to show through the scumble. This causes a pleasing color vibration. Take time out now to practice glazing and scumbling with casein. Make sure each application of color is dry before adding another coat. The wet-in-wet and dry brush methods can also be used in casein painting. Try these, too.

SOME EXPERIMENTS

Set up a pleasing arrangement of colored bottles on your table. Take a piece of illustration board, 18 x 24 inches, and divide it in half so that you have two areas, each of which is 18 x 12 inches. Fix the paper securely to your drawing board. Quickly and freely sketch the still life with pencil in each area. (Don't bother with detail. You can paint that in later.) Now spray the pencil sketches with fixative or clear Krylon Spray so that the pencil will not mix with the casein. While waiting for the fixative to dry, arrange the colors on your palette, get fresh water, select your brushes, rags, etc. All set?

Paint the first still life wet-in-wet. Work quickly. The contours and volumes of the bottles must be painted while they are wet — as in watercolor. Brush in the light and shade. Add the highlights. When this is completed, paint in the foreground and background.

The second still life will be done in dry-brush technique. Set out fresh paint, clean your brushes and refill the jar with clean water. You will paint the bottles in three values — light, medium and dark. First paint the bottles in a flat manner using the medium tone of the glass for color. After this is done, dry-brush your shading on each bottle. Now dry-brush or scumble in the light areas of each bottle. Add highlights. Treat the background simply so that it doesn't detract from the importance of the bottles. There is no hurry. Take your time.

Compare the two caseins you have just painted. Which did you enjoy more — the wet-in-wet method or the dry-brush one? Which was more successful artistically?

COMBINING MEDIA

Ink and oil paint are two media that can be compatibly combined with casein. Try painting casein over and under black India ink and then oils.

CORRECTING

The simplest way to make a correction on your casein is to paint over the faulty area. But if you have been using the wet-in-wet method, first moisten the surface. Then with your bristle brush, scrub out the unwanted part and repaint while the paint is wet. This is not easy to do, but success comes with perseverance.

Varnishing

If you want your casein painting to resemble an oil, give it a coat of damar varnish. Or you might prefer

REGATTA by Mayo Sorgman. Casein.

to use Dorland's Wax Varnish. A varnish should not be applied until the casein has thoroughly dried — let us say in about two days' time. This coat of varnish may be either brushed or sprayed onto the painting. It should be done with extreme care in a very thin layer. Use a large red sable brush for varnishing. Wide horizontal strokes are best for obtaining a smooth coat.

Matting and framing

You may frame your casein painting with or without a mat. I recommend that you eliminate the mat if you have varnished the casein and it resembles an oil. Keep the frame in harmony with the painting. Remember, a person should look at the *painting* first and not the frame. If someone exclaims "What a beautiful frame," then there is something wrong — either the frame is too important for the painting or the picture was poor and not worth framing to begin with.

Be critical of your work! Control your ego. Do not frame everything you do even though Aunt Mary wants to hang it in her den. Just tell Aunt Mary you are waiting to give her something better. I remember how embarrassed I used to be when I discovered some of my early paintings (?) hanging in peoples homes ... !

I shall now paint a cityscape using the wet-in-wet technique and an abstraction using dry brush. Watch the difference. (These are some personal ways of painting. There are many others.)

2. Large areas of darks and lights

1. Sketch

3. Line drawing added

1. Sketch

2. Major dark areas

3. Light areas

(Finished painting on following page.)

4. Dry-brush added

You HAVE learned to use several media. The time has come to be adventurous — to combine two or more media in a single painting. Textures and effects that are unusual and beautiful can be obtained by using the mixed-media technique.

Though mixed-media is popular today, it is by no means new. For centuries artists have combined media in their paintings. During the Renaissance and Baroque periods it was common practice to put a watercolor wash over an ink, pencil or charcoal sketch, to paint oils over tempera, or oils over gold leaf.

Since today's artists are bound neither by academic standards nor techniques, they are inclined to be more experimental in their work. Contemporary artists are breaking all barriers! In fact, when viewing a current exhibition, it is sometimes difficult to decide whether a work of art is a painting or a piece of sculpture. The Spaniard, Tapies, and some of our Pop artists — Jasper Johns, Claes Oldenburg, Robert Rauschenberg and Jim Dine — often cover their painting surfaces with plaster, gesso, cement or other materials to build up relief surfaces. These are then painted over with a variety of media.

Materials and equipment (**use any you have**)

Media
> Oils
> Casein
> Crayons
> Pencils, 4B, 2B, 2H
> Oil stains
> Watercolors
> Tempera
> Inks of all kinds
> Shoe polish

THIRTEEN

Mixed-media for adventure

Mixed media: watercolor, ink, crayon by Karen Van Dyke, high school student. (*Scholastic Magazines*, New York.)

Pastels, chalks
Gouache
Charcoal
Colored tissue paper
Any product to give texture

Brushes

Red sable, round, Nos. 3 and 9
Red sable, flat, 1-inch square end
Bright bristle brushes, ¼ and ½ inch
Bamboo brushes
House painter's brush, flat, 2 inches

Other Painting Tools

Rags
Twigs
Broom straws
Brayers
Sprayguns
Knives or razor blades
Sponges
Toothpicks
Awls
Combs

OFF THE COAST by Lyonel Feininger. Watercolor and ink, 1942.
(*Whitney Museum of American Art*, New York.)

Pens
String

Painting Surfaces

Canvas	Watercolor papers
Gesso panels	Illustration boards
Masonite panels	Newspaper
Charcoal papers	Cardboard (corrugated, smooth)
Tin	Glass
Plastic	

Adhesives

Scotch tape	Thumbtacks
Drafting tape	Stapler

Water and Turpentine Containers

Rags

Eraser

Drawing Board

Techniques

Among the techniques to use are those already discussed:

Underpainting
Overpainting
Glazing
Scumbling
Wet-in-wet
Dry brush

The paints may be applied with any tool and in any manner you wish — by painting, spraying, dripping, scratching or rubbing.

SGRAFFITO

As I mentioned earlier (page 73), sgraffito is a simple method of creating line when applying an opaque paint over a dry color. While the overpainting is still wet, scratch through it with an awl, a toothpick, a comb or a bristle brush. This will reveal the color underneath. Sgraffito was used many hundreds of years ago by the Greeks for their vase paintings. This technique is still practiced by our potters and ceramists.

MIXED-MEDIA

Here are a number of mixed-media combinations for you to experiment with. Try to invent a few combinations of your own. The resulting paint qualities can be fascinating. You may make washes with one medium, overpaint with a second and then glaze with a third.

WITH WATERCOLOR

Watercolor over pencil, charcoal, ink, chalk or pastel, crayon or printer's ink.

Watercolor over a combination of the above.

Watercolor under one or a combination of the above media.

Watercolor mixed wet-in-wet with ink.

Try the above mixtures on wet and dry, rough and smooth surfaces and see how differently the media act. The type of tool you use for applying the paint will greatly influence the final result. You will find that charcoal, chalk, pastel and soft pencil will mix with the watercolor and create a soft blurry effect with an accompanying graying of color. If you do not like this, spray the media with fixative before you wash over them with watercolor.

Both crayon and printer's ink repel watercolor when it is washed over them. The watercolor rolls right off onto the surrounding areas. I like to use a black wax crayon on rough watercolor paper, apply-

Watercolor and ink

ing the crayon with great pressure. Then I paint over this with free large washes of watercolor. Try this using wet and then dry papers. Is there any difference in the way the watercolor "takes"? Experiment with dry-brush watercolor over the crayon.

Using a brayer, roll on a background color of printer's ink. Allow this to dry. Overpaint with watercolor. Any success?

Another interesting technique is that of mixing black India ink with watercolor, wet-in-wet.

1. Securely fasten a piece of 12 x 18-inch smooth white paper to your drawing board.

2. Moisten the paper with a sponge or large brush. (Too much water will cause the paper to buckle.)

3. Quickly draw a landscape with the ink using either a pen or brush. (You will find that the wetter the paper, the more the ink will spread and the less controllable it will be.)

4. While the paper is still moist, paint your watercolor over this allowing the colors to blend and intermingle with the ink.

Try a few more paintings and notice the many subtle accidental effects you can capitalize on. If the paper is too wet, the watercolors will be pale and runny. Experiment with a variety of degrees of wetness and with different grounds.

MORE TO DO   Sketch a clown in detail with a 2H pencil on smooth paper. Overpaint with watercolor using small brushes. Next time use soft charcoal on charcoal paper. Smudge in the light and shade with your fingers. Overpaint with watercolor using large brushes.

Again sketch a clown, using chalk or pastel on a rough-surfaced paper. Spray with fixative. Overpaint with black watercolor and a sponge allowing the pastel to show through.

Make other clowns with combinations of the above media.

Now do the clowns *first* in watercolor and *then*

BREAKWATER by Inez Johnston. Casein and ink, 1952. (*Whitney Museum of American Art,* New York.)

paint other media *over* them. Any difference? Which do you prefer?

On a piece of rough, moist watercolor paper, paint a cityscape with bright watercolors. While the paper is still damp, add black India ink for accent and detail. See how many kinds of lines you can get with the ink — some sharp, some fuzzy and blurry.

WITH GOUACHE

Experiment with these:

a. Gouache over ink, pencil, charcoal, crayon or shoe polish.

b. Gouache over any combination of the above.

c. Gouache under one or a combination of the above media.

d. Gouache wet-in-wet with ink.

How about painting seascapes with gouache and mixed media? You will find that gouache will not adhere to a thick coat of shoe polish. However, polish over your finished gouache will give it a mellow look.

WITH CASEIN

Now explore this group:

a. Casein over ink, pencil, crayon or oil.

b. Casein over any combination of the above.

c. Casein under one or a combination of these media; casein under shoe polish.

d. Casein wet-in-wet with ink.

Compare the opaque qualities of the casein paintings to those you achieved with gouache. Which is more exciting and spontaneous?

WITH EGG TEMPERA

Now are you ready to explore these?

a. Egg tempera over ink, over oil.

SUBWAY SCENE by Isabel Bishop. Egg tempera and oil, 1957-58. (*Whitney Museum of American Art*, New York.)

b. Egg tempera over a combination of these.

c. Ink and/or oil over egg tempera.

d. Shoe polish over egg tempera (then rub off as much as possible).

e. Black or other colored egg tempera over firmly applied crayon.

Make sure that each medium is thoroughly dried before you paint another over it. Mixing other media with tempera, however, does destroy tempera's typical character. It is difficult to differentiate tempera from gouache or casein when using mixed-media. Thick coats of tempera tend to flake off. Black tempera over crayon drawing will cause a "speckled" quality.

WITH OIL

Now let's try:

a. Oil over ink, pencil or charcoal. (Spray pencil and charcoal with fixative.)

b. Oil over pastel and chalk. ("Fix" pastels or chalks before you overpaint.)

c. Oil over gouache, casein or tempera. (Wait until paints are thoroughly dry before you overpaint. Use a *separating* coat of damar varnish before applying the oil paint.)

d. Black ink over oil paints.*

e. Tempera or casein over oil paints.*

f. Shoe polish over oil paints.*

    * Make sure oils are dry before overpainting.

OTHER MIXTURES TO EXPERIMENT WITH

Crayon over dried inks and wet inks.

Black and colored ink over crayon

Colored ink over charcoal.

Charcoal over wet ink and dried ink. (Then spray with fixative.)

Chalk or pastel and wet ink.

Chalk or pastel over dried ink. (Then spray with fixative.)

Chalk under crayon.

Work on a variety of grounds and textures. Apply the media with different types of tools and techniques. I repeat, you can spray, paint, drip, print, scratch or rub media to achieve the effect you want. No holds barred. Only you set the limit!

Remember — always apply oil paint to a thoroughly dried ground!

With the other media, however, try working on wet, damp, and dry surfaces and learn what the varying amounts of moisture do to the paints. You'll be amazed.

Framing

It's your choice! Frame mixed-media paintings to suit your individual taste. Refer to the chapter "Framing Your Masterpiece" for further information.

CONCA D'ORO by Seymour Drumlevitch. Oil and Lacquer, 1951. (*Whitney Museum of American Art,* New York, gift of Mr. and Mrs. Roy R. Neuberger.)

Mixed media by Barbara Betczynski,
high school student. (*Scholastic
Magazines*, New York.)

FOURTEEN

Collage and assemblage

SLEEPING FIGURE by Corrado Marca-Relli. Collage of painted canvas, 1953-54. (*The Museum of Modern Art,* New York. Mr. and Mrs. Walter Bareiss Fund.)

Background

IN 1912, two Cubist painters, Pablo Picasso and Georges Braque, experimented with new ways of painting by pasting bits of paper, string and other materials to their canvases, thereby contributing a new textural quality to their work. The experiments of these two painters opened up new horizons to their fellow artists. Soon many of them, including Juan Gris and Jean Arp, began to glue actual objects — such as labels, scraps of wallpaper and cloth — to their canvases. This new method, which was a protest against traditional ways of painting, was called *collage* (from a French word meaning to glue).

A few years later, during World War I, the Dadaists went a step further. Instead of pasting papers and other materials to parts of their canvases, they now created entire paintings from photographs, pieces of wood, fabrics, feathers, wire and other materials. Leaders of the Dadaists were Max Ernst and Kurt Schwitters.

The Dadaists were revolting against the inhumanity of war and the materialistic world. Working with collage they had complete freedom of creating and did not have to adhere to any traditional way of painting either in media or techniques. They could show new realities with new textures and images. They could do away with perspective and time-honored painting methods. At first objects of ridicule, these collages were later accepted as true works of art.

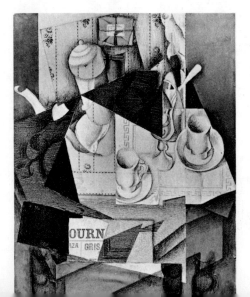

BREAKFAST by Juan Gris. Pasted paper, crayon and oil on canvas, 1914. (*The Museum of Modern Art,* New York. Acquired through the Lillie P. Bliss Bequest.)

138

Today Marca-Relli creates beautiful "paintings" with pieces of rags, or cardboard. Other artists use tin, parts of machines, plastics, pebbles, shingles, glass, beans — or any material — in their paintings. Arthur Dove, Robert Motherwell, Jasper Johns, William Kienbusch, Robert Rauschenberg and Edward Paolozzi are contemporary American artists known for their collages.

In 1961, The Museum of Modern Art in New York held an important exhibition of collages. The exhibition was called "The Art of Assemblage" and created quite a stir in art circles. (You might find a catalog of this show in the library. It contains reproductions of fanciful collages that you will enjoy.)

Despite the unconventional manner in which these collages were executed, they all reflect the basic art principles of rhythm, harmony, balance, unity and texture, though in a new way.

Some people do not consider collages works of art. They feel that paintings must be executed with traditional media in order to be accepted as "true" art. But shouldn't art express the times in which it is created? Should artists have the freedom to create using any subject and any materials they wish? What do you think?

Want to try a collage? There is no limit to the kinds of paint, tools or materials that you can use. In contrast to the rigid, controlled methods of traditional tempera painting, collage allows you unlimited freedom and spontaneity of action. The important factors are ingenuity and creativity!

Start collecting materials — odds and ends, broken items, parts of machines, pieces of wood, ribbon, etc.; gather a real treasure trove of trivia. And all for free! Collect anything that looks interesting in its color, shape or texture. You'll never know when it will be just the "touch" needed to complete your collage. On with the scavenger hunt! Look at the items listed under "Other Media" to start you on the right track.

Materials and equipment

Media
Watercolors
Tempera paint
Casein
Oil Paint
Synthetics
Inks
Pastels and Chalk
Crayons
Pencil
Charcoal

Painting Tools
Red sables
Bristle brushes
Painter's brushes
Rags
Twigs
Brayers
Sprayguns
Knives and razor blades
Sponges

Other Media
String
Dried grasses, weeds
Wood
Parts of machines
Plastics
Fabrics
Dried beans

Materials for collage   (Photo: Nick Verderosa.)

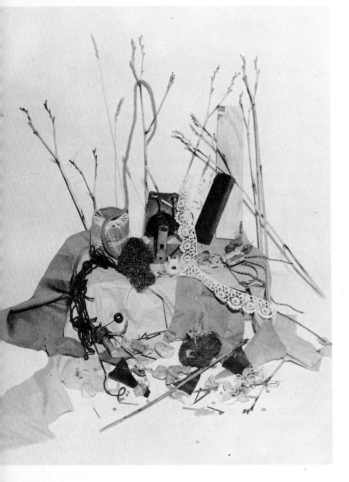

Magazines
Labels
Pebbles
Sawdust
Rice
Seeds
Dime store jewels
Wire
Shells
Wallpaper
Broken tools
Stones
Beads
Bird cages
Eye glasses
Toys
Charcoal
Tin
Glass
You-name-it

Surfaces
Paper
Cardboard
Canvas
Textiles

Plastic
Wood panels
Masonite panels
Tin
Glass
Pieces of wood

Adhesive Materials
Glue
Paste
Drafting tape
Scotch tape
Rubber cement
Solder
Pins
Nails, screws
Epoxy resins
String
Thread
Thumbtacks
Staples, staple gun
Rivets
Elastics
Toggle bolts
Cement
Plaster

Techniques

In working with collage you may paint things — or spray, print, glue, tie, weld, rivet, wire, or sew them, or throw them onto the support or ground.

Happenings

A group of avant-garde artists and sculptors, including Jean Tinguely and Philippe Hiquily, are attempting a new dimension — action and motion. They make arrangements that explode, sculptures that move and paintings that actually drip. These are called "happenings." Exciting things occur to these "works of art" sometimes beyond the preconceived plan of the artist. These happenings are a direct outgrowth of Dadaism's collage and assemblage.

Making a collage

A few paragraphs back, we decided to make a collage. Let's get on with it. You have now collected a variety of things with which to work. How do you start?

First decide — will it be abstract or surrealistic? Perhaps a bit of fantasy? A symphony of textiles? You're not sure as yet?

While you are trying to make up your mind, let's review the following: A collage, like a painting, is basically a composition or arrangement of shapes, lines, colors, and textures. It should have rhythm, balance and unity.

Still not decided? Then let's try this. The subject is "Communication":

Make an abstract using this as a theme. What to use? Torn newspapers, magazine cutouts, large letters to symbolize type, photographs, pictures or actual parts of radios, telephones, TV sets, antennae, telephone poles.... Take it from here:

1. Get a large sheet of illustration board.
2. Select a group of cut or torn paper shapes, large, medium, and small, and arrange them on the board. Make sure you have a variety of color and texture.
3. When you are pleased with the composition, paste it down.

COLLAGE by Susan Diamond, high school student. (*Scholastic Magazines*, New York.)

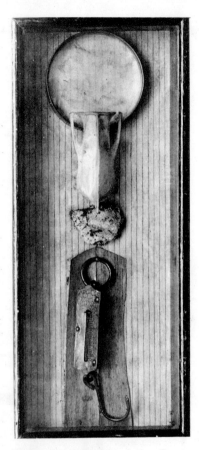

THE INTELLECTUAL by Arthur G. Dove. Collage of objects — magnifying glass, bone, moss, bark and a scale glued or nailed on varnished cloth, mounted on wood panel, 1925. (*The Museum of Modern Art,* New York. The Philip L. Goodwin Collection.)

4. Look through your collection and add other items of interest to the collage.

5. With pencil or paint add necessary lines — sound waves, antennae, etc.

6. Study the collage with a critical eye. Is it interesting? Is it balanced? Does it have unity? Is there a variety of textures? Are there "breathing spaces" (places where the background shows through)? Is the color harmonious?

You may use many materials for the ground. It may be white or colored — spattered, textured, or painted. Weathered old boards, corrugated cardboard or woven sacking make good grounds on which to work.

Your next collage will be "New Year's Eve." Does this conjure up visions of gay streamers, confetti, balloons....?

"High Tide, Low Tide" is another theme to explore. What would you pick up along the beach? Pebbles, shells, colored glass, driftwood, seaweed, pieces of net are a few things to consider using in this collage.

How about "First Snow" as a motif?

The next collage will be a very subtle one — an abstract composed of papers and fabrics of several textures, but restricted to whites and off-whites only. This collage will require careful thought and much planning regarding shapes, textures, and composition. And it will be beautiful!

You will find that working with collage will broaden your viewpoint and stir your imagination. You will become more aware of textures and the relationships of one shape to another and one color to another.

Yes, there *is* something new under the sun — plastic paints! Though they were discovered over a hundred years ago, they were not used commercially until the 1920's. And it is only in the past fifteen years or so that plastic paints have been specifically prepared for artists' use.

Plastic paints are made by combining pigments with plastic (acrylic or vinyl) resins. These resins have great adhesive power. Minute particles of these resins are suspended in water giving the resulting emulsion a milky appearance. This milkiness disappears as the paint dries. When the water evaporates, these resin particles lock together forming a clear film. It is this clear film that binds the pigments.

The word "polymer" is used in referring to the chemical uniting of small molecules into larger molecules. As these molecules enlarge, they become tough and strong. As the resins are polymerized they also change from a liquid to a solid state.

These new plastic paints may be referred to as acrylics, vinyls, polymers or copolymers. Don't be confused with these names as the paints all have similar properties. Most of the plastic paints are water soluble, with the exception of *Magna*, which is manufactured by the Bocour Artist Color Company. Magna is soluble only in turpentine and oil colors. However, for our further discussion on polymers — or plastic paints — we shall refer only to those that are water soluble.

Why are these plastic paints so exciting? For one thing, they are very strong and versatile. They can be used in a transparent manner like watercolors, translucent like tempera, or opaque like oils. They can be underpainted, overpainted, glazed, scumbled or built up into thick impastos. They are non-yellow-

Polymers – space age painting

HOT LANDSCAPE by Mayo Sorgman. Polymer. (Photo: Nick Verderosa.)

ing, adhere to most clean (non-oily) surfaces and do not fade, crack or flake. They are brilliant and reveal a rich depth of color. They dry with almost the same brilliance as when wet. And, too, they can be manipulated with the same tools as those used in oil or watercolor painting.

One of their most desirable characteristics is that of quick-drying. When used thin like watercolor, these synthetics dry almost immediately. If applied thick like oil, they dry within a few hours. This makes them ideal paints to use for outdoor sketching when the transportation of wet canvases becomes a problem.

Another interesting feature of these synthetics is that they may be painted with either mat or gloss finishes. Though these paints are water-soluble, it is advisable to mix them with prepared mediums for best results. These come packaged as *mat* or *gloss mediums*. If you want your painting to have a mat (dull) look, mix the paints with the *mat medium* as you work. For a glossy finish, simply mix your paints with the *gloss medium*. You can mix various amounts of water with either of these mediums to get a desired working thickness of the paint. Since each manufacturer of synthetic paints varies his formulas, read all directions carefully and experiment so that you become thoroughly familiar with the paint before you start a composition.

Because of the rapid drying of the paint, keep your brushes wet at all times while working. Then wash them *thoroughly* in soap and water *as soon as* you have completed your work. Dried paint spells "death" to brushes! And new brushes are expensive.

With synthetic paints it is not necessary to prime your canvas with white lead. Simply brush, roll or knife on a commercially prepared gesso and save hours of work. For building up a relief surface you can buy a prepared modeling paste. Try it for fun!

Polymers come packaged in jars, plastic and metal tubes, squeeze bottles and cans. Visit an art store and examine the various brands.

I recommend the following:

Shiva Acrylic, manufactured by Shiva Artist Colors

Aqua-Tec, manufactured by Bocour Artist Colors

Hyplar, manufactured by M. Grumbacher Co.

Liquitex, manufactured by Permanent Pigments, Inc.

New Masters, by California Products Corp.

Synthetic paints are becoming increasingly popular. A few of the contemporary artists who work with synthetics are Thomas Hart Benton, Ilya Bolotowsky, James Brooks, Elaine de Kooning, Lawrence Kupferman, Theodore Stamos, Rufino Tamayo and Karl Zerbe.

Materials and equipment

(Asterisks indicate basic colors and materials.)

Paints

RED	*Permanent crimson
	*Cadmium red, light
ORANGE	*Cadmium orange
YELLOW	*Cadmium yellow, light
	*Yellow ochre
BROWN	*Burnt sienna
	Raw sienna
	Burnt umber
	*Raw umber
GREEN	*Thalo green

BLUE	*Ultramarine blue
	Thalo blue
	*Cobalt blue
BLACK	Mars black
WHITE	*Titanium white

Brushes
  *Bristle, Nos. 2 and 8 (flats)
  *Bristle, Nos. 8 and 12 (brights)
  *Sable, ¾ inch (flat)
  Sable, No. 9 (round)
  House Painter's brush, 2 inch (flat)

Other Painting Tools

*Painting knives	Brayers
*Rags	Sponges
*Twigs	Combs

Mediums
  *Water
  *Gloss Medium
  *Mat Medium

Supports (painting surfaces). All are satisfactory.

Canvas	Cardboard
Canvas board	Paper
Masonite	Duck
Gesso panels	Burlap (heavy)
Wood panels	

Other Equipment
  *Thumbtacks, or staples with gun
  *Paint box, wood, 12 x 16 inch (or an old shoe box)
  *Palette, a piece of glass to fit the paint box
  Stretcher strips with reinforcement corners
  *Charcoal (medium) and a kneaded eraser
  *Pencil (2B) and a gum eraser
  *Finder, 6 x 8 inches (make your own from cardboard)

(Photo: Nick Verderosa.)

*Water container, anything that holds a quart of water
Stool and easel (portable) for outdoor painting
Table
*Soap
*Prepared gesso
Prepared modeling paste
*Rags

The paints

Polymers are generally in the same price range as oil paints. As with oil, you will use more white than any other color. Because of incompatible chemical properties, alizarin crimson and viridian green are not manufactured in polymers. Instead, a *permanent crimson* and *thalo green* are substituted.

145

To keep the paint moist and fresh, make sure that your containers are tightly closed as soon as you have set the paints out on your palette.

To thin your colors, simply add water or one of the mediums. Once these polymers are dry, they are impervious to water! And once a layer of paint has dried, you can brush another coat over it without hesitation, as the underneath layer will not "bleed" through. Unlike oil, you do not have to paint "fat over lean."

Never, however, mix the synthetic polymer paints with oil or varnish!

All of the colors may be intermixed, but, as with other media, too much mixing will gray your colors. So act accordingly. Clean brushes, clean painting tools and clean water will insure fresh, bright color!

Brushes and other painting tools

As I have suggested, you may use the same painting tools for polymers as you do for painting with oil. But wash your tools carefully *immediately* after using them with soap and water. This is a must!

Try applying polymers with knives, brushes, rags, sponges or twigs and discover for yourself how versatile these paints are.

Painting mediums

Though synthetic paints are water soluble, you may want to mix them with the mat or gloss mediums to keep your paint "buttery."

Experiment by making a small painting using only water as a medium. Then do another painting using only the mat medium. Next use the gloss medium. You'll be surprised at the difference between your three paintings.

Now try painting with combinations of water and mat medium or water with gloss medium. The varying results are many as you will find out.

Painting surfaces

Polymers will adhere to almost any clean, non-oily surface. However, canvas, canvas board, Masonite, wood panels or cardboard should first be coated with a prepared synthetic gesso for best results. This prepared gesso may be applied to achieve either smooth or textured surfaces. Play around with this gesso to determine its possibilities.

(Refer back to the chapter on oil painting for more detailed information about painting surfaces.)

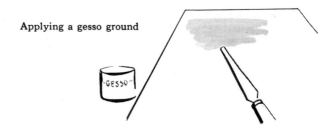

Applying a gesso ground

The palette

The best palette and the easiest to clean is a piece of plate glass. Do not use paper or wooden palettes, as they absorb the water from the paints. Polyethylene ice cube trays also make good palettes. Place a small amount of color in each cube. Wash the tray thoroughly with soap and water when the painting session is over.

Since polymers are quick drying, set out only enough paint on your palette to use within a two-hour period. It is not possible to save the excess paint overnight as it dries hard and cannot be reworked. However, you can extend the drying period by adding small amounts of water to the paint on your palette.

Arrange your palette in the same sequence as you would when working with oil — from warm to cool. Again, refer to the section on oil painting to refresh your memory.

Use the center of your palette for mixing colors and be sure to clean the palette thoroughly with soap and water when you have finished working; otherwise the polymers will dry hard and firm on the palette and will have to be scraped off with a sharp knife.

Experiments with color mixing

When you use the polymers thick, like oils, you can lighten a color by adding white to it. However, should you use these synthetic paints thin, like watercolor, you lighten the color merely by adding water to it. Be cautious here, for too much water may weaken the pigment binder. After you have worked for a while, you will be able to judge the correct amount of water to use.

Here are a few problems for you to solve in color mixing. You may use either a palette knife or a brush for these mixing exercises. (This is a good time to re-read the chapter on oil painting and review the section on color.) The amount of each color you mix will determine the final result.

Experiment by mixing equal amounts of two colors — such as yellow and green. First paint the yellow over the green and then the green over the yellow. Any difference? Now try red and blue, red and yellow, orange and red.

Mix the color of a faded red sweater, a rock in the woods, the bark of a tree, an egg, the sole of your shoe or your little finger.

In nine steps paint a sequence of orange squares ranging from black-orange to white. (This is a hard one, especially when you try to mix dark orange.) If you're really courageous, try this exercise with yellow.

Paint a cold gray November sky that is ominous at the top and graduates to a faint breath of warmth near the horizon. Try mixing the colors of a "Dagwood Sandwich" — three layers of white and rye bread, ham, cheese, mustard and tomatoes and lettuce. Is it good enough to eat?

And for a truly tough one, paint a crystal ball in which your face is reflected! Had enough?

Techniques

Since the techniques for painting with polymers are so similar to those used in oil painting, I suggest you turn back to page 65 and read on from there. Of course, you may invent techniques of your own if you choose.

As we have said, for all of these techniques, mix your polymer paints with mat medium to get dull surfaces or with gloss medium to make shiny surfaces. Personally, I like to use pure water when working with these paints, and then use the mat or glossy mediums as a varnish to get the kind of finish I want. This is a manner of working you will have to decide for yourself after becoming more familiar with these synthetic paints.

WET-IN-WET

If you paint quickly, you will enjoy working wet-in-wet and can achieve glowing results. Remember, though, that polymers dry rapidly and *cannot* be reworked. For completing a painting in one session, this technique is a good one.

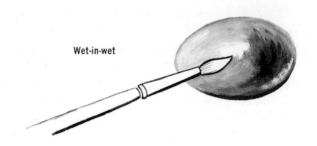

Wet-in-wet

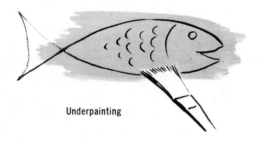

Underpainting

UNDERPAINTING

Because of the rapidity of drying of the polymer paints, underpainting is very simple to execute. There are no long waiting periods before brushing one coat of paint over another. You may underpaint with either thick or thin paint. I do not advise too dark a color for underpainting. Polymers are particularly good for underpainting because they give off a depth and a richness of color.

GLAZING

Here again, polymers are a natural! You can lay one glaze upon another without waiting, as the glazes dry almost immediately. You can glaze a warm color over a cool color, or vice versa. Try starting with a very light color and darken your glazes as you work, layer-on-layer. Glazing contributes an enamel-like quality to your painting. It is particularly successful if you mix the gloss medium with your colors as you glaze.

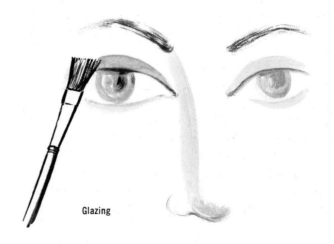

Glazing

SCUMBLING

As you recall, scumbling is the opposite of glazing. You scumble a lighter color over a darker one and use thicker paints. (It is also possible to glaze *over* scumbling. Play around with this technique!)

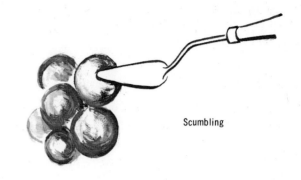

Scumbling

IMPASTO

This term is given to the application of thick paint to create a relief surface texture. Unlike oil, polymers will not crack, so you can build up a thick impasto without fear.

SGRAFFITO

Polymers also lend themselves to this method of scratching through an overlay of wet impasto to reveal the color beneath. You must work quickly and scratch through the surface before the polymer solidifies. As with scumbling, you can get interesting textures and colors by glazing *over* the passages of sgraffito.

Impasto

COMBINATIONS

It is entirely possible to mix these techniques in one painting. You will discover exciting results by doing so. Here is an opportunity to be completely free. Happy adventure!

CORRECTING

Because of the rapid solidifying action of polymers and their great adhesiveness, it is most difficult to remove previously painted passages. For best results, simply paint over an area that you wish to correct. But make certain you use the same medium as in the original painting. If you have many corrections to make, it is much easier to discard your painting and

Sgraffito

start over again. If your painting looks "worried," patchy or overworked, throw it away or hide it in a very, very dark corner!

Varnishing

If you have mixed your paints with either the mat or glossy mediums as you worked, it will not be necessary to varnish the completed painting.

But, if you want your painting to look duller or glossier, give it a coat or two of either the mat or gloss medium. Allow the medium to dry between each coat. Don't be alarmed if your painting acquires a milky surface. The medium will quickly dry out into an invisible film. Caution — never use ordinary varnish over synthetic paints.

Now that you have all the information to get started, why not tackle a landscape or an abstract? As we said early in the book "The Time is Now!" So let's go!

Study this step-by-step sequence as I paint with polymers. (Finished painting on page 152.)

1. Sketch

2. Underpaint

3. Overpaint

4. Glaze

5. Accent

(Finished painting on following page.)

THE WHITE FLOWER by Mayo
Sorgman. Polymer. (Photo: Nick
Verderosa.)

Once you have completed several good paintings, how shall you prepare them for hanging? It is true that the proper frame can make your painting look important, while an unsuitable frame may overwhelm and detract from your masterpiece which, of course, would be disastrous!

When you look at a painting and think, "Why, what a terrific frame!" then the framing is poor. It is the painting itself and not the frame that should attract your eye. Proper framing should be flattering to and compatible with your painting, but it should never "steal the show."

I have seen second-rate paintings appear much better than they were because of the complimentary manner in which they were framed. (Not that you are second-rate, but you know how great you look when you're all dressed up.) Set off your painting with the proper mats and frames. Good framing is creative and epitomizes good taste.

I'm sure you have seen beautiful canvases that were strangled and smothered by frames that were too wide, too heavy, too bright or too ornate. A good frame should do these three things:

1. Protect the painting and separate it from the background on which it is hung.

2. Harmonize with the painting.

3. Add a note of quality and distinction to the painting.

From now on, use these standards as your framing check list! Slip-shod framing with laths that do not meet at the corners, or poorly cut, sloppy mats cheapen any painting.

What to mat — what to frame

"If it's water-soluble, mat it — otherwise, frame it."

Framing your masterpiece

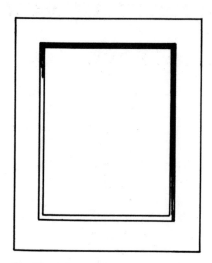

Double mat

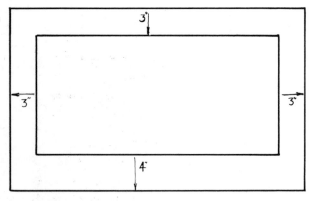

Proportions

This is a good rule to follow; though, like every other rule, there are exceptions.

Usually if you have made a painting in watercolor, gouache, casein, or egg tempera, it calls for a mat, particularly if the painting was treated in a transparent, spontaneous manner. If you made the painting opaque and heavy like an oil, however, then it could be framed without a mat. You are the one to make the final decision! When in doubt as to what looks best, experiment by temporarily framing first with and then without a mat. It will then be easy to make a choice. I usually have a few old mats and frames in my studio that I use for this "testing" process to help me visualize the final framing effect I want.

MATS

Mats are really frames, most often of cardboard (sometimes covered with a fabric), that are used for pictures in all media except oil or polymer. They are a natural for watercolors. They may be made in a variety of textures, colors and thicknesses. Like frames, mats should protect and separate the painting from the background on which it is hung and enhance the quality of the painting by furnishing it with an air of importance. Mats should "hold in" a picture. They should always be compatible with and subordinate to the painting itself. A white, off-white or neutral-colored mat is usually the safest to use. But experiment and see!

Sometimes a handsome effect may be achieved by using a double mat. This usually calls for a white mat exposed under a gray one creating a narrow white insert within the gray mat. However, a double mat is expensive, since you use two mats — one within the other. But the end result may merit the cost.

Proportion

A good mat should be in proper proportion to the painting — neither too small to look skimpy nor too large to lose the painting within its mass.

A good general rule is to keep the top and sides of the mat the same width and make the bottom wider. By cutting a mat in these proportions, you place the painting in a pleasing optical position.

An attractive proportion for a large watercolor (18 x 24 inches) is a mat four inches wide at the top and sides and five inches wide at the bottom. Or you may prefer to make the mat three inches wide on the top and sides, and four inches wide at the bottom. Naturally, smaller watercolors call for smaller mats. But keep these proportions in mind. I might suggest here that you make a few cardboard mats in several sizes and proportions and then try them on your paintings.

Usually windows are cut in a mat and the painting is placed underneath. However, I have seen some watercolors attractively mounted on top of the mat, capitalizing on the uneven edges of handmade watercolor paper.

Color and texture

In addition to the correct proportion of a mat, the color and texture are very important. As you remember, a white, off-white or neutral mat is usually the most successful to use. The color and texture of the mat must not "fight" with the painting but should bring out its luminosity and brilliance.

A painting done in line or in monotone with lots of white or unpainted areas might sparkle in a colored mat. On the other hand, a colored mat could be ruinous to the average watercolor.

A dark mat might overwhelm a delicate painting and "wash out" any subtle areas, so be careful of too great a contrast between the mat and the painting.

Study your painting! Is it predominantly warm or cool, is it bright or neutral, does it have broad or detailed areas? Now carefully consider what effect your mat will have on the painting. A warm colored painting looks best in a warm, creamy mat — a cool painting, in a gray mat. A low-keyed painting is dramatic in a white mat. What mat for a high-keyed painting? You answer this one.

Now for texture. You can buy textured mats, or you can make them by covering cardboard with a fabric such as burlap, monk's cloth, or linen. Textile covered mats usually look very distinguished and elegant. You must be careful, however, in the choice of texture. If your painting is busy or has great detail, use a smooth surfaced fabric. If your painting is bold, broad and free, then a textured fabric might be the best to use.

Start collecting fabrics for future use. Roll them to avoid wrinkling.

Materials and equipment

(Asterisks indicate basic materials.)

*Cardboard	Burlap
*Mat boards	Antique satin
Muslin	Velvet
Linen	Pongee
Monk's cloth	Japanese rice paper
Grass cloth	Beaver board
Marbelized papers	Homosote
*Yardstick	Upson board
Steel square or	*Pencil
metal straightedge	

*Sharp knife,
   Stanley No. 199 or
   X-acto
*Scissors
*Drafting tape, ¾
   inch; or Scotch
   Tape ¾ inch; or
   gummed paper tape
   ¾ inch
*Window glass

Non-glare glass

*Rubber eraser

*Elmer's glue or good
   library paste
*Old flat 1 inch brush
*Rags for cleaning

MAT BOARD

Ordinary white cardboard may be used for matting, but for professional results buy mat board at the art store. Mat board is available in a variety of colors, sizes, and textures. It comes in single (⅛ inch) and double thickness. You can purchase mat boards in sheets ranging from 22 x 28 inches to 40 x 60 inches. These are easily cut into any desired size.

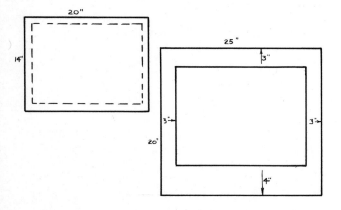

Mat board is made with dull or glossy surfaces and smooth, pebbled, and linen textures. It also comes in a variety of colors. I use single thickness, pebbled mat boards that are white on one side and cream on the other, or white on one side and gray on the other. I find that these are the most flattering to my watercolors. Bainbridge mat boards are excellent.

HOMOSOTE, UPSON BOARD, BEAVERBOARD

These soft composition boards are found in most lumber yards in 4 x 8-foot sheets. Buy them ½ inch thick. (The lumber dealer will cut them into the sizes you need for your mats.) These boards have interesting textures and may be used as mats with or without frames. They are quite handsome if you bevel the inner edges of the window. You may paint the beveled edges white and the rest of the mat any color of your choosing. Rubber-base or vinyl house paint may be either brushed or rolled onto these composition boards. They dry flat and one coat usually covers adequately. You can do professional looking, decorative framing with composition boards. Try working with these materials and discover their possibilities.

MEASURING AND CUTTING

You have painted a beautiful, horizontal watercolor 14 x 20 inches you want to mat. How large should the mat be? First we must decide on the size of the window through which the watercolor will be shown. The window should be at least one inch smaller in each direction than the watercolor. This now changes the dimension to 13 x 19 inches. Suppose we plan on a mat that is 3 inches wide on the top and sides and 4 inches wide on the bottom. Mathematically we now get 19 + 3 + 3, or 25 inches for our horizontal and 13 + 3 + 4, or 20 inches for our vertical dimension. Agreed? Fine — we need a mat 20 x 25 inches.

Using a yardstick and pencil, measure these dimensions on a piece of mat board and then cut with a sharp knife against a metal straightedge. (I suggest you get some help here to prevent blood shed, someone to hold the straightedge firmly in place while you concentrate on the cutting.)

Follow these suggestions:

1. Always use a sharp knife.

2. Use an old piece of cardboard under the mat as you work, to allow you to cut firmly without worrying about scratching the table surface.

3. Practice cutting on the left-over pieces of mat board so that you will soon be able to cut a clean edge and stop your knife at a given point.

4. Angle your knife against the straightedge so that you get a beveled edge as you cut.

You now have a piece of mat board 20 x 25 inches. Next, rule the window space, 13 x 19 inches, on the mat board and carefully cut this out with a sharp knife and straightedge. (Be careful not to run over the corners while cutting.)

Angling the knife. (Photo: **Nick Verderosa**.)

Matting

Now place the mat over your watercolor and move it around until you are satisfied with the placement. When you are sure the mat is in the correct place, put a pencil dot on the watercolor at each corner of the window.

Remove the mat.

Take two strips of drafting tape about 2 inches long and insert one strip at an angle under each top

1. The cut mat

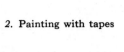

2. Painting with tapes

3. Painting
taped to mat

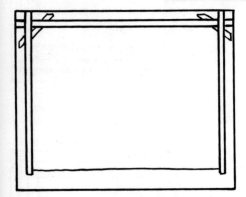

4. Matted
painting

corner of the watercolor paper so that the tape protrudes beyond the edges of the paper.

Take the mat and gently place it over the watercolor, making sure that the pencil marks and corners of the window coincide.

Press down on each top corner so that the drafting tape adheres to the back of the mat.

Now turn the mat *over* and apply drafting tape or gummed paper tape along the top and sides of the watercolor. Let the bottom hang free. (Never use rubber cement for this, as it dries out quickly and may stain the paper.)

How does it look?

Covering the mat

Handsome mats may be made by gluing fabrics onto cardboard or Homosote. Muslin, linen, monk's cloth, burlap, velvet, pongee and antique satin are available in many colors and textures that can be used for this purpose. I recommend that you use neutral shades with a mild textural interest. Otherwise your mat may vie for attention with your painting. (Japanese rice papers and marbelized papers also make attractive mats.)

Covering mats is not difficult, but don't expect perfect results the first time you try. To be trite, "Practice makes ... !"

But let's see how to cover a mat with a fabric (pages 159-160).

If you apply cloth to Upson Board or Beaverboard, make sure you allow enough fabric to fully cover both the beveled window edges and the thick outer edges.

Assembling a matted picture

After the painting is matted, it should be properly

COVERING A MAT WITH FABRIC

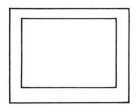

1. Cut a mat with a window from cardboard.

2. Cut a piece of fabric 3 inches larger than the mat. Lay the fabric on the table, face down. (Make sure the table is spotlessly clean and there are no wrinkles in the fabric.)

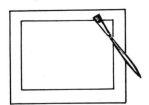

3. Brush Elmer's Glue-All over the entire surface of the mat. Avoid lumps.

4. Place the mat, glued side down, in the center of the fabric and press.

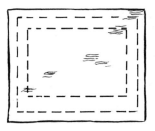

5. Turn the mat over to see if the fabric has adhered to the mat and to smooth out any wrinkles.

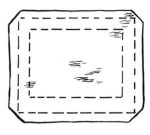

6. Cut off the corners of the fabric. (Careful here!)

7. Turn the mat over again and glue down the excess fabric onto the reverse side of the mat. Pull the fabric tight and smooth as you glue.

8. Here's the ticklish part: Cut out the center of the fabric, leaving about 1 inch of cloth to fold all around the window.

9. Being very careful, slit the fabric at the window corners like mitre joints. (Use a sharp razor for this.) Glue down.

10. Pull excess fabric around the window and glue down on the reverse side of the mat.

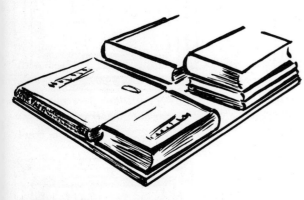

11. Place a clean drawing board and weights (books) over the finished mat until it is dry. You now have a good looking textured mat!

framed. (Sometimes a mat of Upson Board is pleasing enough to stand on its own without a frame.) Glass is usually placed over the mat and then both the matted painting and glass are framed in wood. Make sure the glass is absolutely clean — no fingermarks, dust, or dirt!

It is often difficult to hang a watercolor in a home because of reflections from lighting fixtures. A non-glare glass is available to eliminate these reflecting lights. However, this non-glare glass is expensive and changes the quality and color of a painting.

A watercolor or pastel framed under non-glare glass resembles an oil painting, and because of this I do not recommend its use.

After the matted painting has been placed under glass, it should be framed and then backed with a piece of heavy cardboard secured to the frame with small brads. Now paste a sheet of brown wrapping paper over the entire back of the frame to seal out dust. Add screw eyes and wire, and your painting is ready for hanging. (For more information on assembling pictures, look ahead to "Assembling an Oil Painting," page 162.)

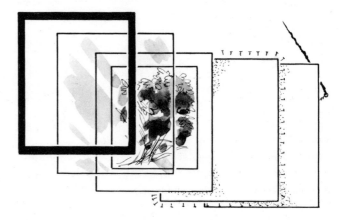

FRAMES

Like mats, frames may be made in various colors and textures, but, unlike mats, they are usually made of wood.

You can easily make your own frames by buying molding at a lumber yard, sawing it to size using a mitre box and then gluing and nailing it together at the corners. But because of the limitation of space, we will skip the building of frames and concentrate on several finishes that may be helpful to you. (By the way, Macy's in New York City sells knock-down frames in many sizes that can be assembled by you in a matter of minutes.)

You can buy raw-wood frames at an art store and finish them yourself, or you can refinish an old frame you have in the attic.

Liners

For a particularly pleasing effect, a liner or insert is sometimes used. A liner is a narrow molding that is placed within the frame to separate it from the picture. Liners are usually painted a color different from the frame — white or off-white — or are covered with a neutral fabric.

Frames can be made of oak, walnut, wormy chestnut, birch or pine. (Of course, the harder woods stand up better.) Some abstract paintings are framed in stainless steel or aluminum.

A frame may be painted, stained, pickled, sprayed, gold leafed or waxed. The choice is yours! Experiment with several of these finishes or combinations of them to see what exciting results you come up with.

Let's discuss the finishing of raw wood frames. You can also use these finishes on old frames once you have removed the paint with paint remover, sandpaper, and steel wool. Ready?

Texturing

You may want to texture your raw wood frame. This may be done by changing the surface of the wood with files, awls or paint scrapers. Always work with the grain of the wood. You can make your texture as subtle or as distinct as you wish. Practice using the above mentioned tools on scrap pieces of wood until you have made a series of textural effects. Be careful of using too much texture. This will give your frame a "worried" look.

Finishing

Before applying any finish to a raw wood frame, it should first be thoroughly sandpapered, rubbed with steel wool and then wiped with a soft cloth to remove any residue. Then, if you want to seal the grain, give it a very thin coat of white shellac mixed with turpentine. When this is dry, rub the surface with fine steel wool until the wood is smooth.

STAIN FINISH

Making a stain finish is very easy. First, decide on the kind of oil stain you wish to use and then thin it with turpentine until it lightens to the desired shade. (You can make your own stains by using oil paint thinned with turpentine.) Soft woods like pine take stains easily. Their open grain absorbs the stain quickly. Hard woods take longer for the stain to penetrate into the wood fibers.

ANTIQUE FINISH

1. Sand and steel wool the frame.

2. Give it a coat of white casein paint.

3. When this is dry apply a thick coat of white enamel paint, brushing it smooth as you work.

4. Allow it to dry.

5. Brush on a coat of turpentine-thinned burnt sienna. Rub off immediately with a dry cloth.

6. Brush on a coat of thin raw umber and rub this off with a dry cloth.

7. Add more burnt sienna or raw umber to suit your taste. Wipe off.

8. If you wish, you may wax the frame when it has dried.

PICKLE FINISH

This is particularly good for wormy chestnut or any textured wood surface.

1. Brush on a thick coat of white oil paint.

2. While still wet, rub off with a dry cloth. (The white paint will remain deposited in the crevices of the wood leaving only a thin tone of white on the smooth surfaces.)

3. You can add another color over this and then wipe immediately. (Here, again, you should practice on scrap wood.)

4. Effective results may be obtained by darkening the corners and edges of the frame.

5. When dry, add a coat of paste wax.

Assembling an oil painting

Attaching the canvas to a frame is a simple matter requiring only one-and-one-half-inch brads and a hammer. Here goes:

1. Put the frame, face down, on the table.

2. Insert the canvas, face down, into the frame.

3. (You will find that the canvas and stretcher protrude above the frame, so angle a brad and nail it through the stretcher and into the back of the frame.)

4. Put the first brad through the center of the top stretcher piece. Now put other brads through the center of each of the other three stretcher pieces. Your canvas is now fastened to the frame.

5. Continue adding brads 6 inches from the center of each stretcher piece, working toward the corners of the frame. And that's all there is.

Now that the painting is framed, how do we hang it?

1. Keep the painting face down on the table.

2. Using an awl, punch a small hole about 6 inches from the top on both vertical stretcher pieces.

3. Insert a screw eye in each hole and turn until it is securely embedded in the frame. (Use a pair of pliers to help you tighten the screw eyes.)

4. Cut a piece of picture wire one foot larger than the width of the frame.

5. Insert the picture wire across the back of the frame through both screw eyes. You will now have 6 inches of wire protruding from each screw eye.

6. Twist this extra wire around each screw eye and then around the long wire.

7. Your wire is now firmly secured.

8. Now find an auspicious place for your painting and hang it so that the *center of the painting is on your eye-level*.

You can buy picture hooks at any hardware store that will support paintings of various weights. Do not use paste-on hangers because your picture may crash to the floor once the adhesive of the hanger has dried out. Happy hanging!

Painting for a hobby

PAINTING HAS been practiced as a hobby by some of the most famous people in the world, including the late Prime Minister Churchill and ex-President Eisenhower. It is extremely satisfying and offers you opportunities to truly express your ideas. You don't have to follow the crowd, for your individual uniqueness will be your passport to the world of art.

Exhibiting

After you have become proficient in painting, there will be opportunities to exhibit at schools, in the local libraries, museums or in community art fairs that are held in the spring or fall. Most times your work will be judged by a jury of artists before it is accepted for hanging. If you don't pass the jury, don't be discouraged. Re-evaluate your painting to see why it didn't come up to the jury's standards. Then work harder to make a better painting.

It is sometimes difficult to judge a painting because it is such a personal thing. Juries have individual likes and dislikes. A painting that passes one jury may be turned down flat by another. (Recently a painting of mine received a national award. I entered it in a local art show and it didn't pass the jury!) Don't try to paint an "exhibition picture" or in the style of another artist. Paint what you wish in your own way. Be true to your convictions. Recognition will come in due time.

After you have painted for *several years,* you may want to try exhibiting in regional or national open shows. These shows are all juried. Hundreds or thousands of paintings are entered from which only a small number will be chosen.

SEVENTEEN

Looking ahead

(Photo: Nick Verderosa.)

Usually there is a fee (not-returnable) of from $2.00 to $10.00 for each painting submitted. This, plus crating and express charges, makes exhibiting at one of these shows expensive. Some of the larger national art shows require color slides of your work. If these are acceptable, you are then invited to send the actual paintings.

A few of the larger exhibitions you may inquire about are the Audubon Artists Show, The Allied Artist Show, the American Watercolor Society National Show and Watercolor U.S.A. If you are adventurous and firmly believe your paintings are wonderful, by all means try to enter these shows. *Art News*, *Arts*, and *American Artist* magazines each month print a list of regional and national shows. Consult them for further details.

All artists dream of having a one-man show in New York City — the center of the art world. When the proper time comes and when your work is good enough, you can make the rounds of the art galleries to inquire about a one-man show. Or, better still, your work may be seen at an open exhibition, and you may actually be *invited* by a gallery to have a show. Send me an invitation to the opening!

Contests and scholarships

Scholastic Magazine each year holds state and national contests for high school students. Seniors may submit portfolios of their art work to be judged for scholarships to leading art schools and colleges. Ask your art teacher for further information or write to Awards Director, *Scholastic Magazine*, 50 West 44th Street, New York City.

Most art schools provide full or partial scholarships to talented students who are in need of financial assistance. To apply for a scholarship, simply write to the art school of your choice and submit a portfolio of your best work. Your portfolio should contain from eight to ten examples done in a variety of media. The judges will look for originality, creativity, and good drawing. It might be wise to include a naturalistic self-portrait or a meticulous drawing. All of your work should be neatly matted to show it off advantageously! You might also include a letter of recommendation from your art teacher or high school principal.

For those of you on the college level, there are many opportunities for scholarships for post-graduate study such as the *American Academy in Rome* fellowships, 101 Park Avenue, New York City; the *Fulbright Art Awards,* Institute of International Education, 800 Second Avenue, New York City; and the *Ford Foundation Fellowship Program for Creative Arts,* 477 Madison Avenue, New York City. Consult with your college art department for other scholarship opportunities.

Vocations in art

Now that you have enjoyed success working with many media, have you decided to become an artist? Is this the only career you want? Then an artist you should be!

But first you must climb down from the clouds and realize that the road to an art career is a long and arduous one. It requires much study, perseverance and downright hard work. Today's artist doesn't paint in a garret and wear a beret. He is a hard-working (but happy) citizen. He must accept responsibilities, meet deadlines, be subject to many pressures and continually produce excellent results.

Some positions in commercial art pay very high salaries. This field is very competitive, but there is always room at the top for a good man (or woman, of course). Remember, only a handful of artists in this entire country are able to support themselves through the sale of their "fine art" paintings.

Here are some of the vocations in the world of art. Read the list carefully, select what appeals most to you, and follow through!

COMMERCIAL ART

Art buyer	Fashion artist
Art director	Illustrator
Book designer	Layout man
Calligrapher	Medical artist
Cartoonist	Package designer
Color consultant	Photographer
Cover designer	Portrait painter
Display artist	Scientific illustrator

INDUSTRIAL DESIGN

Architect	Package designer
Automobile designer	Photographer
Ceramist	Product designer
Color consultant	Renderer
Fashion designer	Store designer
Furniture designer	Stylist
Model maker	Textile designer

INTERIOR DESIGN

Architect	Merchandise buyer
Ceramist	Refinisher
Color consultant	Stylist
Fabric designer	Upholsterer
Interior decorator	Weaver

MUSEUM WORK

Art curator	Photographer
Display artist	Researcher
Lecturer	Restorer

STAGE AND TELEVISION

Color consultant	Makeup artist
Costume designer	Photographer
Letterer	Set designer
Lighting technician	Graphic artist

TEACHING

Art consultant	Art professor
Art critic and commentator	Art supervisor
Art historian	Art teacher

Interior, The Solomon R. Guggenheim Museum, New York City. (Courtesy: *The Solomon R. Guggenheim Museum.*)

Art schools and colleges

For a career in art, attendance at a good art school or college is usually a must.

In almost every community there are art classes sponsored by Adult Education, the local museum or art guild. Take advantage of these classes and learn as much as possible from your local art instructors. I'm sure you can find afternoon, evening or Saturday morning art classes somewhere in your vicinity.

As for art schools and colleges — this is a list of those I consider outstanding in specific areas. There are many other good art schools. See your art teacher or consult *Art Career Guide* by Donald Holden, (Watson-Guptill Publications) for a more complete list. Write for catalogs and carefully study their contents to be sure you are fully qualified for acceptance.

This is a key to the numerals:
1 Fine arts (painting and sculpture)
2 Commercial art
3 Industrial design
4 Interior design
5 Museum work
6 Stage design
7 Teaching
8 Crafts
9 Photography
10 Architecture

8,9	Alfred University, Alfred, New York
2,3,4	Art Center School, Los Angeles, California
2,3,4,7	Art Institute of Chicago, Chicago, Illinois
1	Art Students League, New York City
1,5,7	Bennington College, Bennington, Vermont
1,7,8	Boston Museum School, Boston, Massachusetts
2,3,4,7,8	California College of Arts and Crafts, Oakland, California
1,3,6,7,10	Carnegie Institute of Technology, Pittsburgh, Pennsylvania
2,3,7	Cleveland Institute of Art, Cleveland, Ohio
4,7	Columbia University, New York City
1,2,9,10	Cooper Union, New York City
1,4,10	Cranbrook Academy of Art, Bloomfield Hills, Michigan
5,10	Harvard University, Cambridge, Massachusetts
2,3,7,10	Illinois Institute of Technology, Chicago, Illinois
7	Iowa State Teachers College, Cedar Falls, Iowa
1,4	Kansas City Art Institute, Kansas City, Missouri
7,8	Kutztown State College, Kutztown, Pennsylvania
1,7	Massachusetts College of Art, Boston, Massachusetts
7	Montclair State Teachers College, Montclair, New Jersey
4	New York School of Interior Design, New York City
1,7,9	New York State University Teachers College, Buffalo, New York
1,5,7,9	New York University, New York City
4,6	Northwestern University, Evanston, Illinois
2,5,7,8,10	Ohio State University, Columbus, Ohio
2,3,4	Parsons School of Design, New York City
1	Pennsylvania Academy of Fine Arts, Philadelphia, Pennsylvania
2,3,4,7,9,10	Pratt Institute, Brooklyn, New York
1,2,3,4,7	Philadelphia Museum College of Art, Philadelphia, Pennsylvania
2,3,4,7	Rhode Island School of Design, Providence, Rhode Island
2,3,4,8	Rochester Institute of Technology, Rochester, New York
2	School of Visual Arts, New York City
1	Sarah Lawrence College, Bronxville, New York
5,6,7	State University of Iowa, Iowa City, Iowa
1,3,7,9,10	Syracuse University, Syracuse, New York
1,10	Tulane University, New Orleans, Louisiana
2,3,7	University of California at Los Angeles, Los Angeles, California
5	University of Chicago, Chicago, Illinois
6	University of Colorado, Boulder, Colorado
1,2,7,10	University of Illinois, Urbana, Illinois
5,7	University of Wisconsin, Madison, Wisconsin
1,7,10	Washington University, St. Louis, Missouri
2,3,4,7	Wayne State University, Detroit, Michigan
1,5,10	Yale University, New Haven, Connecticut

On to a glorious career in the arts!